Advance Praise

"A great read! The quotes throughout the book create a time for pause and reflection. Not only for what has happened in the past, but for what truly can be possible today and beyond. It is within that inner reflection that we create the best outward version of ourselves. Denise totally captures this in her book."

– Sandy

"Denise's book and her coaching have been fundamental to the success I've had in how I process my emotions and the way I feel about myself. She's knowledgeable, empathetic, and truly cares about the people she helps."

– Graham

"Denise has a very special gift. I am so grateful to have had the opportunity to learn from her. Through her guidance, I have developed a new self-awareness and many techniques to help me live my best life. I highly recommend her book and her guidance through the use of the tools she shares."

– Raylene

"My life drastically changed for the better when Denise came into my life. Her book is a reflection of the new perspective on my relationships and she shared with me how to have the difficult conversations that were necessary for me to grow and make improvements in my day-to-day life. I'm forever grateful."

– Lisa

"Wow, what a great book! I can relate to going through a divorce in a small town, and Denise has a way of explaining concepts and ideas in a way that I have never considered before. As she states in her book, it is our struggles and our heartaches that shape us the most. Her book gives us hope that we can come out on the other side of our struggles with more confidence, greater strength, and a resilience to overcome adversity."

– Sonia

"I met Denise when I was in the throes of my divorce, and as a result of working with her, I was able to move forward with greater confidence and hold my head high in the process. Her book is the perfect complement to her coaching practice. She coached me down a very difficult path and I am very appreciative of her knowledge, practices, and her genuine love."

– Jen

"Men sometimes approach consultation with apprehension, fear, and anger. Applying the techniques in her book and working with her personally, I felt very comfortable opening up to her about my marriage. I was able to discover new insights and perspectives that changed how I saw myself and my situation."

– Mark

"You do not have to be from a small town to be able to relate to what Denise shares in this book about gossip and others talking about your life. I love the fun and helpful tips that she suggests on how to become the best you that you can be through the movie she calls life. Love is all you need; let the rest of the stuff go."

– Quinelle

"Denise shares a friendly, straightforward approach in being able to not only survive but thrive through our day-to-day experiences. She reveals what it is like to be real and raw, and the vulnerability that comes with that. She lends a helping hand and provides a road map to guide you down the road as you learn to hold your head high through it all."

– Shanna

"I love how Denise shares her intimate, hilarious and vulnerable stories through her journey of self-discovery after divorce. I felt powerful, inspired, and capable as I read through [each] chapter. I love how the steps in this book can be translated to all aspects of our lives. Brilliant. Just brilliant!"

– Tasha

SMALL TOWN DIVORCE

Small Town
DIVORCE

A ROAD MAP THROUGH
Devastation, Despair,
AND *Drama*

Denise J. Anderson

NEW YORK

LONDON • NASHVILLE • MELBOURNE • VANCOUVER

Small Town Divorce

A Road Map Through Devastation, Despair, and Drama

Published in New York, New York, by Morgan James Publishing in partnership with Difference Press. Morgan James is a trademark of Morgan James, LLC. www.MorganJamesPublishing.com

ISBN 9781642797862 paperback
ISBN 9781642797879 eBook
ISBN 9781642797886 audiobook
Library of Congress Control Number: 2019913391

Cover Design by:
Rachel Lopez
www.r2cdesign.com

Interior Design by:
Christopher Kirk
www.GFSstudio.com

Editor:
The Author Incubator

Book Coaching:
Cory Hott

Morgan James is a proud partner of Habitat for Humanity Peninsula and Greater Williamsburg. Partners in building since 2006.

Get involved today! Visit
MorganJamesPublishing.com/giving-back

For my boys, Evan and Ethan, who inspire me every day with their warrior spirit and zest for life! Thank you for being my greatest teachers, my inspiration, and the two people I love and cherish the most.

Thank you to Angela Lauria and The Author Incubator's team, as well as to David Hancock and the Morgan James Publishing team for helping me bring this book to print.

Table of Contents

Foreword

*S*mall Town Divorce is a fascinating journey that moves well beyond the compelling and thought-provoking reflections, the raw, heart-breaking experiences, and the often laugh out loud, small town absurdities one experiences in navigating the labyrinth of divorcing in close-knit communities.

Frankly, when I was asked to read the book, I did not know what to expect. I'm a man who experienced divorce in a moderate sized town; I was twelve years down that road— been there, done that, and got the t-shirt. But as I read the book, I was stunned to realize that not only did it apply to my experience directly, but this book applies to *everyone* who has experienced divorce.

Within massive cities like San Francisco and New York, the same dynamics Denise Anderson outlines plays out in exactly the same ways within the microcosms of apartment complexes, burrows, and suburban neighborhoods. I could relate to it all and it caused me a significant regret.

My regret stemmed from the fact that I did not have this book in my tool bag to help me move through the challenges I faced within my own "small town" experience with more ease and grace. I believe having these validating reflections would have eased my journey, but it goes well beyond the power of feeling better. There is deep wisdom in this book that would have saved me time and energy, and made me not feel like I was a fish out of water, desperately gasping for breath, as I tried to move forward in my life.

To be a great coach, the single most important skill is the ability to listen, really listen to the needs of the client. A coach must also possess a true empathy and deep respect for what the client's needs are in moving toward their goals and desired outcomes. An outstanding coach possess that perfect balance of not solving problems, but rather leading the client to their own discovery so they are empowered to move forward in their lives, while also holding the client accountable to agreed-upon action steps. It is a delicate balance that requires adaptability and a strong intuition, along with not judging others in any way, shape, or form for their struggles through the process. Lastly, an outstanding coach must be the client's biggest fan, a genuine supporter of them achieving their aspirations.

These qualities are a rare find in the world of coaching, and Denise Anderson embodies all of these elements to the highest degree. I spent twenty years in law enforcement and, frankly, I am hard to impress, nor do I give endorsements lightly (because my professional reputation is on the line). In this case, I have no problem referring Denise to anyone. They will be—beyond question—in good hands.

Small Town Divorce: *A Road Map through Devastation, Despair, and Drama* is a literal road map through devastation, despair and drama—a journey where you will likely laugh, cry, and jump up and down in triumph. Denise Anderson is an amazing writer and life coach, and if you or a loved one find yourself in the throes of divorce, this is a must read.

Rodger Ruge

Host of HeroTalk (HeroTalk.org),
Human Potential Life Coach,
Certified Stress Management Practitioner,
and Master Instructor.

Chapter 1

Break Up in a Small Town

*"Living in a small town
is like living in a glass house."*
– Mallika Nawal

"Oh my Gosh, have you heard?" Kim asked Pam. "Jack and Dianne are getting divorced!"

"What? You have got to be kidding me," said Pam.

"I'm not kidding. Bob told David at work this morning."

"What happened?" asked Pam.

"Well I overheard Lynn down at the coffee shop this afternoon telling Martha that Dianne was screwing around," said Kim. "But when I went to the grocery store, I heard Jim whispering something about Jack not being faithful, so I'm not exactly sure."

"Wow, I can't wait to tell Betty. She can't stand Dianne. She will know exactly what went down with whom, and you can bet that she will have all of the other juicy details as well."

"Oh, I already told Betty," said Kim. "Our kids go to playschool together, so I mentioned it to her when we were picking up the kids just before lunch. The teacher, Ms. Thatcher, had already heard, as well, but she heard that Jack wasn't happy at his job and that he had been taking money from the company for several years," said Kim. "Apparently they had been having marital problems for quite some time now.

"Betty and I went for lunch together at the new restaurant on Main Street afterward and our waitress confirmed the rumors about Dianne," Kim rambled on. "Apparently, Joan and Cheryl had been in there eating, and Cheryl said that everyone at the post office was talking about it. I highly doubt that Cheryl will stay friends with Dianne if the rumours are true. However, I am not really sure if it's

Dianne's fault because when I stopped at the liquor store to grab a bottle of wine for dinner tonight, the ladies there were actually upset with Jack, so now I don't know who's leaving whom! I know that man is no angel. It is driving me crazy trying to figure this out. I will get to the bottom of this situation one way or another.

"What I do know is that it is all over town," Kim said with a gleam in her eye. "Chris said she heard that the word on the pew after the church service on Sunday was that Dianne actually had another man on the go, and that she may even be pregnant! Could you even imagine at her age? What in the world was she thinking?"

"Well, I am going to head home and see if Harry has heard anything down at the car dealership," Pam chimed in. "I know that Jack can be extremely ornery at times, and that temper of his would have Mike Tyson shaking in his boots. I have seen Jack jogging around town in the mornings, so I wouldn't doubt that he is up to something, you know? You can bet that we will find out more information at the kids' hockey game tonight. That rink is a cesspool of gossip, rumours, and overt opinions. No doubt that whirlybird Wanda will be there pronouncing the gospel truth in between every fried burger and deep-fried mushroom that's served."

4 | ***Small Town*** Divorce

"Well, I really hope that Donavon hasn't found out yet because he's best friends with Jack. A bit of a loose cannon, if you ask me. Oh, and wait until the in-laws find out," Dianne said with a Grinch-like grin on her face. "The sky is going to light up like the Fourth of July! And if that girl ain't running for the hills yet, she better be saying her prayers because once this gets out into the oil patch, it's gonna make Hiroshima look like a campfire!"

"Gather around folks—it's about to go down!" concluded Kim as she strutted across the street, into her car and drove away feeling like she had accomplished her day's mission.

If you are from a small town, you may be familiar with this type of dialogue. Divorcing in a small town is its own special circus. There are hoops to jump, tightropes to walk, trapezes to swing on, sharp knives to juggle, magic tricks to perform, many clowns to deal with, and a lot of fire to be eaten. You need a badge of honour just for surviving the experience.

Finding yourself smack dab in the middle of a circus ring can be quite concerning. I want to offer you some hope of getting out of that ring and leaving the circus behind. There is a light at the end of the road you are traveling. This book will serve as your road map to navigate your way down that long and winding road. You will face obstacles along the way, and there will be many challenges, as well. It is difficult to stand up to your adversaries and to deal with all the gossip in town. I want you to know that there is hope. There is a way to free yourself from all the drama, and I will be with you every step of the way.

Your divorce is out in the public and now it is up for public debate. I heard recently that a friend of mine was divorcing from her husband. They were together for almost twenty years. As the news spread, the questions on everyone's minds were, "What happened?" and "Why are they getting a divorce?"

People go into detective mode and insist on finding the real cause of the situation. They act as though they will find the evidence needed to prove the reason for the demise of that marriage or relationship. And once they present Exhibit A to the jury, it's all over. I hope that my friend is able to rise above the inevitable investigation, and that she and her husband will be given some space and compassion to feel their way through the ending of their relationship.

Divorce is a dramatic, life-changing experience that involves a lot of heartache and pain. Unfortunately, this fact is often overlooked, and people use it as an opportunity to shame, blame, judge, and criticize. You lose friends as sides are chosen and judgment is passed. You are watching your children go through a very painful experience as they watch their parents' divorce. Your heart is breaking for them as you do your best to love and support them through it. You have a lot of changes to deal with all at once, and it is overwhelming and scary. Uncertainty is a constant, and it is easy to be consumed and overtaken by fear. Thoughts continually run through your head, making you doubt everything about yourself.

And if all of that isn't enough for an individual or family to deal with, you get the added bonus of other people's opinions, comments, and snide remarks about your separation, and there isn't any aspect of your relationship that is off limits. Sides are taken and you find yourself on the outskirts, or your spouse is the one taking the hit. Either way, one of you must be the bad guy and, like it or not, you will be the main topic of conversation down at coffee row for weeks or months on end.

Your main goal is to just make it through the day. You hope to be as inconspicuous as possible while you perform your daily errands, trying to avoid conversations that may lead to someone inquiring about the details of your divorce. You easily recognize the people that have taken your side, and it is even more evident to you the ones who have not. You can't seem to get off of the emotional rollercoaster that you are on, and your mind and thoughts will not let you have a moment's peace. We will find that peace for you and get you more comfortable on that the rollercoaster you're riding. You hope that when you put your head on your pillow at night, all of your limbs are intact, and that maybe tomorrow, you will be able to work through the feelings and the process of your divorce rather than losing energy to the drama and details that others are so interested in. You dream of a day where you can walk through the streets, hold your head high, and just move forward. That, my dear, was why I wrote this book. We will have you holding your head high by the time you are done reading this book, as long as you promise to play along with the suggestions I give. I will be here if you need any additional help.

You are paying a high price for staying in this constant state of turmoil. You can't sleep at night, which makes it difficult for you to handle your emotions. You are uncertain about many of your friendships. You question who is actually concerned about you and who is more concerned about getting a few more juicy details. The uncertainty gives way to a lot of anxiety and stress, which isn't helping you to move forward. The constant talk around town deflates and immobilizes you. You have no desire to attend any social events, and the thought of facing people at the grocery store makes you want to throw up in your mouth. Your energy is low, and you fear of falling into a depression, if you haven't already.

An acquaintance of mine, who was separated from her husband, was unable to shop for her own groceries or go anywhere near downtown without having a major panic attack. The thought of having to face people, of having to talk about her divorce or of having to endure the looks and glances of others was enough to send her over the edge. The constant attention and drama were just too much for her. Her divorce was tumultuous enough, but the added public display was more than she could handle. She suffered for a very long time with this anxiety and experienced other health complications and relationship issues because of it.

I know that going through a divorce, especially one that others have decided to become a part of, has no doubt taken its toll on you. To continue carrying the weight of others' opinions will stop you from experiencing or expressing yourself in the many creative ways you desire, too. You may have picked up some unhealthy habits to help ease the pain and unsettling emotions that you feel on a daily basis. These habits may be affecting your health and the way you feel about yourself and may also be interfering with your performance at work. Your fear of the unknown has you settling for a comfortable solution that does not necessarily serve you or light you up.

My friend, Amanda, was overwhelmed by the drama she experienced in her small town when she divorced a rather prominent and popular man. As he held a position of authority and respect, the townsfolk did not take too kindly to her leaving the marriage and them having to see this man go through a lot of emotional upheavals. She was ostracized and judged. She endured a lot of harsh looks, rude comments, and the constant reminder that people were not happy with her. No one really had all of the information of what was really happening for this couple, yet they took it upon themselves to make her life as miserable as possible.

Despite the dismal outlook that your days may hold, there is an opportunity for you to go beyond the chaos of your day. I want you to know that it doesn't have to be this way, and that there is hope for your situation to improve. There is also an opportunity to get off of the emotional rollercoaster you are on and experience your days with much more calm and ease. I will share some helpful hints that you can incorporate into your daily experiences that will help you to move on and catch a glimmer of light at the end of the road you are traveling. Imagine if you could face all those rumours and people who act as though it is their life's mission to take you out of the game? Facing your greatest fears, quietening that self-doubt, and healing those broken relationships are all possible for you and may, in fact, be just around the corner.

I have outlined eight activities in this book that will serve to support you in working through the challenges and drama that you have faced going through your divorce in a small town. As I mentioned earlier, divorcing in a small town has its own special flavour. On top of your divorce being discussed publicly on the daily, you are trying to wrestle with all of those thoughts in your head that continually try to convince you that you aren't good enough. I will share some tidbits on how to make friends with that voice in your head and with those voices you hear on the outside. You have also had the misfortune of living your emotional turmoil publicly, which just seems to add more fuel to the fire that is already burning inside of you. I have a few buckets of water you can use to lower the flames on that fire without having to endure any third-degree burns. It is difficult to go through it alone, and the challenge is real. I hope that you can have some fun with this, despite the craziness that you are experiencing. I am here to help and guide you through it, as I have weathered and overcome this same experience. So, snuggle up, get cozy, and let's dig through this dark tunnel and find the light that is waiting on the other side.

I want you to know that so many opportunities await you on the other side. As you are able to increase your courage and self-worth, possibilities for you and your life become endless. Experiencing a greater connection within your relationships lends itself to experiencing deeper and greater love than you have ever known. Improved physical and emotional well-being brings forth a wellspring of energy that benefits not only you, but everyone around you. And, of course, letting go of the things in your life that no longer serve you will allow you to meet someone very special: The real YOU!

Chapter 2
I Didn't Know My Own Strength

*"Character cannot be developed in ease and quiet.
Only through experience of trial and suffering
can the soul be strengthened, ambition inspired,
and success achieved."*
– Helen Keller

I sat with my friend one morning over coffee and told her that I had something I needed to tell her. I shared with her that my husband and I were separating and would be getting a divorce. It was something that had been weighing on me for a long time, and I wanted to share the news with her before she heard it from anyone else. I knew that once it went public, people would be asking what happened, what went wrong, and more importantly, whose fault is it? In truth, it is no one's fault. I know most people won't want to hear that. It is not as exciting as finding out the juicy details of my relationship, and it certainly will not get me on stage at the Jerry Springer show or a write-up in the *National Enquirer*. Trust me, all you need to do is to start dating someone who has gone through a divorce, and all you hear is their crazy ex-wife story or their jerk of an ex-husband story. Don't worry, I played that game as well. No one wants their right to tell incriminating stories about their ex to be taken away from them. I am not about to do that. I will, however, offer an opportunity to go beyond the drama, all the drama.

Opening up about my divorce and having that conversation with my friend was very difficult. Undoubtedly, telling my two boys what was happening was beyond heartbreaking. I knew that the news was going to crush them, and that there was a long road ahead for us to travel. There were going to be many obstacles that we would need to overcome, a lot of emotions that we would need to process, but there was never a moment that I questioned our ability as a family or as individuals to overcome and work through this experience.

Like most, I certainly didn't walk down the aisle with the intention or thought that this would all end in a divorce one day. We went on from our wedding day to have two amazing boys. We had numerous business ventures. We traveled, and we enjoyed participating in as many outdoor sports as possible. We were a very active, engaged, and lively family. People were trying to make sense of our separation as some feared that if we could get a divorce, the same could happen to their own marriages.

What I experienced was that a lot of people became more interested in the dirt than they were in understanding and having compassion for what was happening. A family was going through a life-changing event as traumatic and emotionally challenging as experiencing a death would be. People wanted to start pointing fingers and make someone out to be the bad guy, and they wanted to find out the cause for what was happening. It is easy to start spewing stories to appease the people's curiosity and to ease your own pain as well. As with any highly emotionally charged event, we want to find out what we believe is causing all of this pain and make it stop. More often than not, the first questions a person will ask after hearing that a couple has separated is, "Whose fault is it?" I will go into more detail on the dynamic of this question in Chapter 4 when I address the gossip floating around town. Needless to say, my divorce was emotionally challenging and was a very difficult time for the entire family.

As for anything that happens in a small town—once the word gets out on the street, it is open season! The gossipers do not need a license to go for the kill. No species is off limits, and they can use any weapon they choose. They don't spend too much time trying to decide which weapon will serve them best, for it's right at the tip of their tongues. There are very few weapons that can be deployed that cause as much damage as the words from one's mouth. They penetrate more deeply than any shiny bullet, and their effects last longer than any gunshot wound takes to heal. You have within you a weapon capable of causing mass destruction, for when your words intertwine with the already existing doubts, fears, and uncertainty that lie within your target, you have a potent formula I feel is comparable to chemical warfare. And let's keep one thing in mind: I am not talking about the children who are bullying other children on the playground. There is no pink tee shirt day to bring awareness to adult bullying because we don't actually call it that in this situation. We call it gossiping, small-town chatter, and whispers down at coffee row. It is all completely legal, and without a doubt, justifiable, because you are getting a divorce and they know what you did last summer!

However, just like the young bully on the playground, we must ask ourselves, what is that bully trying to achieve lording over the other children? We conclude that the bully must not feel that great inside about himself if he feels the need to assert himself over another being. Perhaps, he may have even done something himself that he doesn't feel so great about, but if he can focus everyone's attention on the shortcomings of someone else, that will take the heat off of his own deeds.

The minds of many are drawn to adversity and drama, and divorce in a small town is a breeding ground for this very thing. Shortly after the news came of my own divorce, a good friend of mine sat down with me. She took it upon herself to let me know how she felt about me, my situation, and my actions, and then she proceeded to tell me that we were no longer friends. I was quickly introduced to the fact that people would be volunteering their views on me and my marriage, without any notice. Until that moment, I thought that people were more interested in volunteering on the local school board, volunteering to coach little league, or volunteering for the town-wide Dickens Festival. Apparently, there are many ways we can volunteer our *services*. I learned to be ok with the friends that were no longer a part of my life. I had many friends who loved and supported me, so I focused on who was by my side rather than getting worked up about who wasn't.

I wonder if people would be so eager to offer their opinions on you and your divorce if they knew that, once they were finished going through your life with a fine-toothed comb, you then get to go through their life, their sex life, or lack thereof, and the way they have treated others, with the same feverish aptitude. I cannot imagine that people would buy into this, but then again, do you really need them to? They didn't seem to ask anyone's permission to dive into your life, your shortcomings, or publicly discuss your human disposition. I will let you in on a little secret though if you are interested? The words, judgments, and other profanities you wish to inject into the person you feel is so deserving of your tongue lashing won't come close to the lethal injection of self-blame, self-shame, and self-hatred that that person is injecting into themselves.

While going through my divorce, the one song that I would listen to over and over again was *I Didn't Know My Own Strength* by Whitney Houston. I knew that, in order to get back on my feet and to be able to hold my head up high once again, I was going to need to dig deep and find out what

I was made of. The song was a source of inspiration, and it still is today. I listen to that song when I need to remind myself that I got through all the pain and that I found my own strength.

"Lost Touch with My Soul."

Ouch! Lost touch with my soul? Sounds serious. Well honestly, it felt that way. I wasn't sure who I was anymore. Life was not turning out the way I had planned, and I became frightened, uncertain and, quite frankly, a little lost. I defined myself as a "wife" for so long that I really didn't know who I was without that title. Sure, I saw the same face looking back at me when I looked into the mirror, but it felt like I had lost a big part of my identity, and I wanted to find it again. Little did I know that I was embarking on a much larger task than I had originally set out to do. The search proved to reveal something much greater than a title or label could provide. By placing my own personal life coach in my corner, devouring books and applying their message, and absorbing as much wisdom and positive energy that was available to me, I was able to work through many of the tough truths I needed to face. However, my own will, desire, and determination to learn and grow from this experience proved to be the number one factor that changed everything for me.

"Thought It Would Be the End of Me."

You know that moment when you are at the end of your rope and you can't distinguish one body part from another? Well, I had one of those moments, except that moment lasted for many months. When you live in a small town, you become accustomed to people knowing your business, or at least taking some pretty uneducated guesses about your business.

But after a while, it becomes physically and mentally exhausting. I wasn't able to go anywhere without someone knowing who I was. I couldn't hide! I couldn't head down to the coffee shop, leap over to the dress shop, slide down to pick up some flowers, before I sauntered on down to buy some milk from the grocery store without most people in town knowing what kind of coffee I drank, what dress size I wore, what type of flowers I bought, and what percentage of milk I drank. (I would always switch percentages just to mess with people.) That one block jaunt exposed me to about fifty people, and forty-nine of them knew me by my first name. And this scenario went on day after day after day after day. When I dug a little deeper into what was holding me back, and when I was able to let go of what other people were saying about me, this trip downtown stopped tripping me up, and I started enjoying my daily routine.

"I Thought I'd Never Make It Through. I Had No Hope to Hold on To. I Thought I Would Break."

Sounds like I was pretty fragile, huh? Well, when you are walking through what can best be described as, oh, I don't know, one of the lowest times in your life, it is easy to feel fragile and breakable. I did feel like I had been broken into a million pieces. Even though I was the one to initiate the divorce, it did not lessen the pain of the experience. And once again, having the divorce being publicly discussed made a difficult situation even more difficult. It felt as though there must be something wrong with me at the core of my being if I could not make my marriage work.

Working through this challenge was no easy task. I didn't have a road map. Where the heck was Google Maps when I needed it most? Not even Google or the most sophisticated navigation system could help me get out of this. I will share with you in this book the road map that I did find and end up using to walk my way out of the unending emotional turmoil, put my mind at ease by questioning the most negative and self-limiting thoughts that arose, and allow myself to face anyone who challenged me. Some good old eye contact and speaking up for yourself goes a long way in growing your confidence.

"Survived My Darkest Hour."

I didn't want this event in my life to define me or to deter me from becoming the best version of myself. Working diligently on those thoughts in my head and finding a new way to experience my emotions allowed me to open up to so many new possibilities. I used the same techniques in this book to complete my first marathon with just thirteen days of training, pass my mutual fund exams, start my own coaching business, and write my first book. I am not perfect, but I have certainly made peace with this woman I call Denise, and I feel extremely honoured that I get to support others in finding this for themselves as well.

"I Crashed Down and I Tumbled, but I Did Not Crumble."

It is so important to remember that everyone is traveling their own unique path, and that no one's journey is free of stumbles and tumbles along the way. What brings about those tumbles, how far down the rabbit hole you may fall, and regardless of how many times you crash, the most important thing is how many times you get back up. I love the quote from the movie *Rocky*, "It ain't about how hard you can hit. It's about how hard you can get hit and keep moving forward!" I want to equip you with the same right jab, left hook and lights-out uppercut I used to fight my way back to the top and never look back.

"Hold My Head Up High... I Was Not Built to Break; I Didn't Know My Own Strength."

What doesn't kill you makes you stronger and stand a little taller. Even throughout those dark nights of the soul and moments spent sprawled out on the floor, there was a voice inside of me whispering to wake up, look up, and get up. Coming face-to-face in those moments with not only the people in my town, but with the voices in my head, I was able to pick myself back up, hold my head up, and find a strength inside of me that I never knew I had.

Chapter 3

One Step Away From the Dance of Divorce

"Over every mountain, there is a path,
although it may not be seen
from the valley."
– Theodore Roethke

The dance of divorce is diverse, turbulent, and very intimate, and calls upon your ability to navigate your way through the challenges and obstacles revealed to you along the journey. You are not alone on your journey. I will share with you a road map that you can follow to help find your way out of the drama, confusion, and uncertainty that you find yourself in. I will help to quiet the noise around you as you attune to your own rhythm and begin dancing to the beat of your own drum.

The path of finding your own rhythm is not carved out in stone, and neither is the path in this book. Feel free to turn to the chapters that most intrigue you and engage in the fun suggestions as you feel inspired to. As you relate to any of the stories shared along the way, please feel free to reach out and share your own experience with me.

To make it easier for you to remember the fun suggestions that I have given in this book, I created an acronym. I call it the D.I.V.O.R.C.E.D dance. I will outline what that stands for so you will know what lies ahead in the following pages.

D—Decide Whose Opinion You Value

This will help you to disengage from all of the gossip and unsolicited opinions that everyone around you seems to be sharing on a regular basis. When you are clear about whose opinion does matter, you will easily dismiss the opinions of those who don't.

I—Invite New Friends

Most friendships do not last a lifetime. You have likely already experienced many friends who have turned away from you and who are no longer in your circle now that you and your spouse are not together. Take a look into the lessons and gifts that you received while being in these relationships, and then let it go.

V—Value Adversity

The adversaries you have come to face have no doubt provided extremely challenging moments for you. Trust that these challenges are helping to build the necessary muscles to help you grow. We will build upon the resistance provided by your adversaries to help you hold your head high and move forward with greater confidence.

O—Overcome Emotional Resistance

There are many ways to get lost and consumed by your emotional up and downs. No doubt you have experienced your fair share of emotional turbulence throughout your divorce. Allowing yourself to feel whatever feeling arises will help you to overcome any tendencies you have to guard or protect yourself. You will come to know that you are safe, and no harm will come to you.

R—Retrain Your Brain

Introducing new daily habits and routine can change the way your brain processes thoughts, and therefore how you respond to your environment. If you keep doing what you have always done, you will keep getting the same results. I know you are tired of the endless chatter in your mind and the effects this constant nattering has on you. Let's get some fresh new data into your mind, and set that hamster in the wheel free.

C—Change Your Perspective

An overwhelming amount of change has been brought into your life in a very short period of time. Finding comfort and safety in your new environment can be difficult. Challenging the idea you have about the way things are supposed to be rather than the way they are will help you to find some peace of mind. Looking for the positive things that are showing up in your new environment will help to provide a much-needed reprieve from your longing for things to be the way they used to be.

E—Engage in Conversation

Your desire for connection and healing is a natural part of the divorcing process. Wanting to reconnect and rebuild certain relationships and your desire to feel more connected again after feeling so alone is natural and necessary. You may feel vulnerable as you open yourself up to others through honest and real conversations. You will become more comfortable over time as you share what is in your heart with those you love.

D—Develop Self-Love

The greatest gift you can give anyone is the gift of love. Coming to know yourself as love rather than defining yourself based on thoughts, emotions, and events you have experienced will elevate your life to the next level. A joy will arise in you that is not dependent on your life's circumstances looking a particular way. You have this natural feeling state inside of you, and it is your time to experience it.

We will go through each of these steps together as we develop your skill of riding the emotional rollercoaster. I know that temperatures are on the rise, and it is easy to lash out. However, there is a way for you to feel intense emotions like anger, frustration, or pain, and not lose complete control of your senses. We will also enhance your ability to face your fears with as few skid marks on the inside of your shorts as possible (there is no guarantee, of course, so keep the toilet paper handy).

And how about getting through that dense forest of end-less thoughts running around upstairs in your head? I bet you would love to take an ax to all of those nasty, negative thoughts roaming around in there. You know, those pesky little rodents up there, nattering comments and trying to convince you that you are the worst parent ever, that you always screw up, that you are not worthy or lovable, and that nobody likes you anyway. Yeah, those ones. I don't want you believing those thoughts any longer. You know that they are not serving you, and they will only make you feel even worse about yourself. I will give you an antidote to counter-act those thoughts, which will turn you in a new direction and have you seeing your world from a new perspective.

I want to make this as fun as possible for you, so think of this as a road map that you can use to navigate your way through your most difficult days. After sharing some of my experiences and what has worked for my clients, I will ask you to have some fun with me. I will have you make some observations. I will give you an opportunity to step into your power. And you will get to have some fun coming up with creative ways to become more comfortable with the change you are experiencing. Who knows, maybe you will run your first marathon, write your first book, or start that business you have always wanted to start.

Although I call it fun, I honour how difficult and painful getting divorced is. I do. Divorcing has taken its toll on you, I'm sure, regardless of whether your divorce took place in a small town, a city, or some other place on planet earth. You will need to tackle that gossip, those adversaries, and the unnerving thoughts. Let's get you proficient in dealing with fear and all of those changes, and let's make you brave enough to have those difficult conversations. I know that any effort or energy you put into this will reward you many times over. You will go from feeling overwhelmed and tired to feeling capable and alive, from feeling afraid and alone to feeling confident and connected. You will be putting my suggestions into practice as you read the book, and I will be available to play along with you when you are ready to take your life to an even higher level. I want to help you hold your head high and live your life from your greatest source of well-being and brilliance, preferably sooner rather than later! Let's get started!

Chapter 4

Whose Bed Have Your Boots Been Under?

*"It is easier to dam a river
than to stop the flow of gossip."*
– Filipino Proverb

"I don't think I can take it any longer," Karissa confessed to me one afternoon when we were driving to the city. "I know that I am not perfect, but I can't even have a coffee with my brother in this town without people asking questions. My furnace breaks down and

33

the neighbours are on hot alert to find out whose truck is in my driveway. Last week, I had a sweet little old lady wanting in on the action, so she took it upon herself to let all of the other little old ladies know that she thinks I might be sleeping with the doctor."

"What in the name of Sam Hill is she talking about?"

Karissa added more to her story before she let me chime in. "Someone even asked me the other day if my ex was dating the new girl that just moved to town, like how the heck would I know what he is doing? Why don't they just ask him?" Karissa sighed and then hung her head in disbelief.

I could feel how much this was affecting my friend. She started to cry. I wanted to say something that would help to ease her pain, but she was too upset to listen to anything that I would say. At this point, she just needs to cry.

Karissa was quiet as she looked away and stared out the window. "I think people have forgotten that we are going through a divorce, not auditioning for The Jerry Springer Show. My family is going through a lot, and it seems as though everyone is more interested in the gossip and telling stories," Karissa stated. "I don't know who they think they are, or what they are trying to accomplish, but this is devastating." Karissa continued, "I wish they would have the balls to come and talk to me directly, but

I doubt that will ever happen." She looked over at me and finished off with a bold statement. "And do you know why I think that will never happen?" Karissa wasn't going to wait for me to take a guess. "It won't ever happen because if they confront me, they would have to take the chance that I may turn to them and ask them whose bed their boots have been under." I let out a laugh to lighten the mood and my friend let her guard down just enough to puff out a meek giggle.

Gossip is a common phenomenon that people going through a divorce often experience, especially in a small town. Well, let's be honest, it is a worldwide epidemic. People love to talk. They just love being the first one to spread the good news about other's mishaps, wrongdoings, and unconscious acts, and what they don't know, they make up! I mean they embellish, exaggerate, and add all kinds of bells and whistles to their elaborate stories. They do not need to get the details very accurate, and they speak as if they know the gospel truth. People like to get to the bottom of things and find out who's been up to what, so the most inquisitive details are often asked as soon as the divorce is out in the open. It is especially noticeable in a small town where conversations about the details of other's lives are often on the agenda for the day's discussions.

Throughout this chapter, I will be discussing the dynamics of gossip that have no doubt touched your life in a significant way, especially while going through your divorce. It is well known that gossip freely flies around small towns, so by the end of this chapter, you will care a lot less about that gossip, and you will know how to face it.

Life in a small town is so different than life in a big city. There are many advantages to a small-town lifestyle that benefit everyone in the community. People come together for a common purpose, whether that is to prepare the diamonds for the upcoming baseball season, to clean up the local swimming pool, to donate to the bake sale, or to organize a fundraising event. It allows everyone to be involved, to give back, to work together, and to make the community strong, viable, and prosperous. I am so grateful for the experience of raising my children in a small town.

However, not all things in a small town are about bake sales and ball games. When it comes to personal events in one's life, living in a small town can take on a much different feel, a much different experience. All of a sudden, the demands of preparing the sports arena, the importance of organizing the local library, or voting for the next town mayor has been put on a shelf. Yes, something much more important is happening. Something much more worthy of people's time and energy. Something that needs immediate attention and air-time. You are getting divorced!

Stop the press! Oh, did I just say, "Stop the press?" I meant to say, "Alert the press." Let's get this on the front page of the newspaper. This news is worthy of the church bulletin, the community flyer, and even the sandwich board on Main Street. This beauty keeps the local folks abreast of all of the events happening in town. Things like big discounts in clothing stores, dates and times of provincial hockey games, various fundraising events, and your divorce! Okay, I have never actually seen a divorce announced on a sandwich board or posted anywhere publicly, but when you are going through one, it might as well be. Seeing the announcement in black and white might feel a little less intense than having to hear the whispers, murmurs, rumours, and gossip running rampant through the streets.

I am going to take a stab at why people might find it so fascinating to talk about other people's lives and the journey of their divorce. Hopefully this helps you to shed some light on the matter and takes away some of the sting you feel from others commentary about you. First of all, if they need to talk about your life in such a way, perhaps they don't have a lot of interesting or exciting things going on in their own life. If they did have it going on, I doubt they would have the time to be concerned about your life. A feeling of insecurity or inferiority can make them feel the need to exert control and power over you, so they spread gossip as a way to build themselves up. Of course, this tactic isn't effective, because they are building themselves up on a very sandy surface that will surely crumble. Here's a big one; they could very likely have something going on in their own backyard that they don't want their neighbors to see, so they distract everyone from the weeds in their backyard by pointing out the weeds in others' yards. Very effective way to deal with things, wouldn't you say?

When Mandy came to me for support, she was going through a divorce that had many people in town talking. Mandy and her ex-husband had recently moved to a new town. Their business venture did not pan out the way that they had hoped, so when it became public that they were divorcing, people were making up all kinds of stories about their failed business, about an extended family member of hers who had had a few run-ins with the law, and people insisted on making up stories about her ex that weren't true. Mandy was a bright, funny, and intelligent woman, but all this town talk was leaving her feeling isolated, afraid, and angry.

She began to withdraw, and soon found that she was unable to go out into public without having major anxiety.

This had a major effect on her emotionally, as well as physically. She needed to focus on her divorce, which happened to be an amicable agreement between her and her ex. She had never lived in a small town before and was blown away by the attention her life was receiving. I asked her if she knew who was talking about her. When she said that she knew exactly who it was, where she lives, and what her cell number is, I knew that Mandy had been well climatized to the small-town environment. I suggested that Mandy have a chat with this woman, either by calling her or speaking with her in person. Mandy was uncomfortable with this idea, but she also knew that she needed to do what she could to put a stop to this. A few days later, Mandy called this woman and told her that she had heard she was spreading rumours about her. Mandy mentioned that she herself had not heard this woman say those things, so she offered her an opportunity to say if she had or hadn't been speaking about Mandy. She admitted to repeating what she had heard at the post office a few weeks earlier. Mandy asked that, if she ever heard anything about her around town, would she please come to her directly with any questions or comments she has about what she heard. Mandy said the woman was very sheepish, but agreed to talk to her directly next time. We don't know if she really will, but Mandy felt so much better after the conversation she had with this woman. It gave her back some confidence and a way for her to handle any gossip about her in the future.

People talking about you, gossiping about you, spreading rumours about you, or sharing things about you that you actually did do or say can be hurtful, to say the least. There are days you just want to go and get a jug of milk, pick up your mail, and watch your children play hockey or perform their dance routine without having to endure the painful sideways glances, the disapproving looks, or ignored conversations. The interesting thing about going through a divorce in a small town is that there isn't anywhere you can hide. You can't go out for a cup of coffee at the local coffee shop, get a burger at the fast food joint, fill your tank with gas, or have a drink down at the tavern without this energy following you. It is like a black, dark cloud following you around, and it makes it difficult just to get through the daily tasks in your life.

You are not alone when it comes to gossip. No man or woman is off limits to the ramblings of others, and the more you do in life, the louder those voices get. Take a look at any well-known actor or actress. The media is filled with the latest goings-on of the who's who and people just lap it up. Perhaps we are now conditioned and accept it as normal and okay, because everyone else is doing it (that's always a good reason, isn't it?). Or, maybe you haven't been informed that chatter about other people is one of the lowest forms of communication that we can engage in. People could be having conversations about new business ideas, about exciting adventures they want to experience, or they could be chatting about creative ideas they would like to explore.

I do want to caution people who believe that they are not affected by the opinions of others. I truly hope that you aren't, but I have met people who are convinced that they really don't care what people think of them or what people say about them. They will proclaim that they don't give two hoots and are completely oblivious to the ramblings of others. But what they have done instead is created a very small life for themselves. They refrain from putting themselves in any position that would lend itself to criticism or opposing views. They keep their circle small and often do not make the effort to meet new people or engage in new activities. It can prevent them from meeting fascinating people, seeking out new opportunities, or discovering some great talent within them. Rather than having to face people who are saying things about them, they shrink, play small, and hide to protect their feelings. They aren't really living their life. I don't want that for you, and I know you must have picked up this book because you actually want to face that gossip rather than run and hide.

This is exactly what I shared with Michael when he called me up to work through a rough period he was going through. Michael is a fun-loving guy and has the biggest heart you can imagine. He loves to make people laugh and is usually upbeat, but not that day, nor had he been feeling that way for a long time. Michael fell into a depression, as there were many things crumbling down in his life all at once. He had always been concerned about his reputation, and as a result, when people started talking about his failing health and financial decline, he realized how attached he was to the opinions of others. It actually caught him off-guard. Because he usually wears a smile and tends to look on the bright side of things, he never imagined that this type of situation would bother him as much as it did.

I explained to Michael that their opinions really don't matter. People are going to say what they are going to say, and that will always be the case. I told him that the amount of validity that he was giving to other people's opinions may end up causing a more serious situation than he was already dealing with. He prided himself on being well off financially. He was able to travel and vacation on a regular basis, and he always kept himself in great shape. It was killing him to have to face others and to hear them talk about his situation. I handed Michael a piece of paper and asked him to write down the names of a few people who he genuinely respected and whose opinions would mean something to him, because he knew their opinions would be coming from love and respect and would be in his best interest. Michael took a few minutes to think and then looked up at me when he was finished writing the names down. I told Michael to carry that paper with him and when someone other than the people on that list offered their opinion, he can nod, allow them their air time if he so wishes, but then he is to dismiss what they have just said. I suggested that he completely let it go if he really wanted to move on from this situation. Michael let it go and found that he had a lot more energy to deal with his financial situation. It took him a while, but he began to feel better about himself. He still works to disregard others' opinions of him, but he has made a lot of progress and was so thankful for the suggestion.

No one has been appointed judge, jury, or executioner over you. No one has authority over you. I understand that it can feel like they do, or that they have the right to judge, but they don't. Not one human being is without wrongdoing or can say that they have never hurt and harmed another person. There is great wisdom in the quote, "Let he who is without sin cast the first stone." If someone is talking trash about you, please remember, and perhaps you can remind them, that no one walking around this planet is perfect. Other people do not get to decide who you are, unless, of course, you let them.

Let's equip you with a hack so you can adequately deal with all of those rumors, gossipers, and unsolicited opinions. This is where I invite you to have some fun with me and play along. This a suggestion that Brene Brown gives in one of her books. The way that I share this with my clients, and how I personally have done this, is by writing down the names of the people whose opinions do matter to you. I am talking about those people in your life who you have a deep respect for, and who will give you an honest and introspective perspective of things. I have four names on that list, and you can bet these people are living large; they don't play from the cheap seats. If you didn't make the cut, guess what—your opinion doesn't matter to me. I always keep that paper handy to remind me of the irrelevance of others' opinions. I cannot stop all of the chatter and gossip, but I know that over time, you will not be affected by their words and that will have a huge impact on your life, it certainly has for me and the people that I work with.

When I stopped allowing people's opinions to matter or personally affect me, I wasn't afraid to express myself; I wasn't afraid to say the things that I needed to say, or to do the things that I desired to do. People are just too concerned about what others think of them that they don't live their lives from truth and authenticity. It is too easy to let someone else's opinion penetrate your mind and allow it to make you question yourself and your dreams. This has happened to so many people that I know, and I don't want that to be you!

Chapter 5

Friends May Not Be Friends Forever

"Some people are going to leave, but that's not the end of the story. That's the end of their part in your story."
– Unknown

"Hey Pam," Kim said into her cell phone. "I know that Jack and Dianne have been going through this divorce for several months now, but every time I see Dianne walking down the street, I just want to turn the other way, you know what I mean?"

"Well, no, I don't know exactly what you mean," Pam replied.

"I just mean that I don't like her," Kim said forcefully

"Well, you used to like her. In fact, you two were very close friends," Pam reminded Kim. "You two have had a lot of laughs together. Your kids are close and you two have supported one another through some really tough times. I don't quite understand where this is coming from."

"Do you really need me to explain this to you, Pam?" Kim said with snark. "You know what she did. You know what she can be like. I am surprised that you are still talking to her, Pam. And besides, you can't be friends with both Jack and Dianne. I mean, how awkward would that be?"

"I don't really have a good enough reason not to talk to her, Kim, and I don't see why I can't be friends with both of them," Pam responded. "Have you talked to her about things? Have you asked Dianne what she is going through? Have you had a conversation with her about how you feel or how all of this is affecting you? I know that she would be open to talking to you Kim, but you are going to have to reach out to her."

"Can I remind you, Kim, that Dianne is going through a lot right now? Just like you, me, and everybody else in this town, Dianne is doing her best. She doesn't always make the best decisions, but neither do you. She doesn't need your judgment right now Kim—she needs a friend.

"I am trying to get you to see what you are doing. Why does everybody think that they have to take sides? Why do years of friendships have to end because a couple is divorcing?

"I understand that people want to support their friends during a divorce, but is ostracizing their spouse the best way they can find to show their support? Dianne isn't perfect and Jack sure as heck isn't either," Pam kept rolling. "Their children are hurting, and Jack and Dianne both are, too. Do you really think that the best way you can contribute to this situation is by choosing sides and shutting out Dianne from your life? And in case you didn't notice, their children are watching and hearing what others are saying about the two people who they love the most and who love them. Have you stopped to consider for one hot minute how your actions and words toward either of their parents are affecting them? Or, have you made this all about you?" Pam knew that Kim needed to hear what she was saying.

Surprisingly, Kim had nothing she wanted to add. Pam hoped that Kim would honestly consider what she just shared. And even if Kim decided to no longer hang out with Dianne, Pam hoped, for the sake of the kids, that Kim would keep her opinion about Dianne away from the children. Pam knew that one day this would all be over, and attempting to go through it from a place of love and respect for all parties might one day be possible.

And so begins the drama of the dispersal of friends. You are no doubt familiar with this game. Your friend list will never be the same, as some friends have chosen to fly south for a permanent vacation from you! We will discuss the division of friends, how one decides if they should stay or if they should go, and what you should do about all of it, if anything. Let's explore what to do with the friends who have turned their backs and left you hanging. You will find a way to come to terms with the way things are with your friends, and you can also decide if you want to invite any of them back.

I am going to guess that if you have been through a divorce, you are no stranger to the process of friends choosing sides. A division of friendship can occur almost immediately following the news of a breakup. Conclusions are drawn, judgments are made, allegiances are pledged, and alliances are formed. And do not kid yourself; it will be made known whose team you are on and whose team you are not on.

How will you know for sure that a friend is divorcing you, you ask? Well, when your friend comes up to you and tells you that she doesn't want to be friends with you anymore, that would be one way to know. Or, if a friend comes and takes back a gift that she gave you, that would likely be a good indication. If your friends are having a party and they don't invite you, you guessed it—you're off the friend list. Or if you walk into a room and they are all huddled in a circle and as soon as they see you coming, they tighten up their circle; face the facts: you ain't in their circle and you ain't getting in. Essentially, if your friend slights you in any way that shows any sort of disrespect towards you, it is safe to assume they are no longer looking out for your best interests. When divorce is occurring, it feels as though every relationship in your life is in question. You are unsure which friends are going to stick by you. You are unsure how your in-laws are going to react, and you may even question how family members are going to respond to what is happening. Mere acquaintances can also come out of the woodwork and offer their support or let you have it.

I had two very important young people in my life who I was not allowed to connect with or to see anymore. I was asked not to buy them any gifts, and I was cut off from all communication with them. It was an extremely painful experience to go through, as I loved them both dearly. Of course, I would have preferred for this not to happen, but it did, so the first thing that I learned was to accept what is. Painful, raw, and sad—it is what it is. I had to sit with those emotions. After that, the only thing left to do was to let go. Fighting against what is happening will throw you further down the rabbit hole and only create more drama. The good news is that many years later, I have these two amazing people back in my life. As painful as it is, it takes time for some relationships to heal and mend. It can feel awkward and difficult to have conversations with people whose relationship you would like back in your life, but remember, relationships do not mend on their own. I will talk more about these hard conversations we need to have later on in Chapter 10 when we dive into vulnerability.

There is a proverb that I would like to share with you as you struggle with the relationships in your life. It will help to shed some light on what you are experiencing, a perspective that may help you to see things from a fresh point of view.

People come into your life for a reason, a season, or a lifetime. When you figure out which one it is, you will know what to do for each person.

When someone is in your life for a reason, it is usually to meet a need that you have expressed. They have come to assist you through a difficulty, to provide you with guidance and support, to aid you physically, emotionally, or spiritually. They may seem like a godsend, and they are. They are there for the reason you need them to be.

Then, without any wrongdoing on your part or at an inconvenient time, this person will say or do something to bring the relationship to an end. Sometimes they die. Sometimes they walk away. Sometimes they act up and force you to take a stand. What we must realize is that our need has been met, our desire fulfilled—their work is done. The prayer you sent up has been answered, and now it is time to move on.

Some people come into your life for a season, because your time has come to share, grow, or learn. They bring you an experience of peace or make you laugh. They may teach you something you have never done. They usually bring you an unbelievable amount of joy. Believe it, it is real. But only for a season.

Lifetime relationships teach you lifetime lessons; things you must build upon in order for you to have a solid emotional foundation. Your job is to accept the lesson, love the person, and put what you have learned to use in all other relationships and areas of your life. It is said that love is blind, but friendship is clairvoyant. Author unknown.

We won't know the reason that someone is in our life or how long the season of a relationship will be, so try not to get too bent out of shape when your friends are picking sides, your in-laws don't want anything to do with you, or you are no longer a part of the cool crowd. As difficult as it is, this dynamic can be a big part of the divorcing process

I know how painful this can be. I don't doubt that you can recall many friendships that have ended or that just don't feel the same since your divorce. It is a real loss that you feel as your circle of friends changes, and you don't participate in the annual events that you and your friends would plan. It is awkward meeting them on the street, and sometimes you are unsure if you should say hi or not. You will not be able to avoid them in a small town much the same way you cannot avoid the office dynamics at work. Everyone is in a small, confined space, and you will have to face your friends sooner or later. You may miss them, and yet you feel like you can't tell them that. You are angry with them for not being friends with you anymore, and you feel you can't tell them that either. And you are sad that the friendship has ended, and you for sure aren't going to tell them that. You just have to trust that there is something shaking out of this for you, and that you will have the people in your life who you are meant to have. Everything reveals itself in its own time.

I once helped my client, Madison, work through what she described as a devastating break up with one of her best friends. The two women had been friends for over ten years, and they shared a lot of laughs and funny shenanigans together. They shared many personal secrets with one another, and the absence of her friendship left a hole in Madison's heart and in her life. I could feel the pain that Madison was in. The friendship came to an abrupt and unexpected ending during Madison's divorce from her husband, and they never mended their friendship. I proposed that Madison write a letter to her friend letting her know how she feels. It was important for Madison to share her hurt and sense of loss in order to move on. She let the tears flow as she recalled all of the laughter and the good times. It was a way for her to honor the relationship before she could let it go. She realized sometime later that the dissolution of relationships is a natural process. No one stays the same; dynamics and needs change as well. She still thinks very fondly of her friend, but they both moved on, and they are both better for it.

Sometimes we leave friendships in haste and sometimes we allow them to linger on past their due date. It is not mean, uncaring, or hurtful to consciously end a friendship whose season is up. You have both benefited and grown in ways that would not have been possible without the friendship you shared. You do not have to wait for a dramatic event in order for you to recognize if a relationship uplifts you or not.

And now for a bit of fun to help you deal with and heal from those broken friendships. Go ahead and take an inventory of your relationships. Which friends of yours are no longer a part of your life? Who do you miss and what would you like to say to them? Write out the gifts you received from this friendship and what you valued the most. See if you can mine out the gifts, the growth, and the lessons you received from each relationship. Make a list or a mental note as you reflect upon that person and the times you have shared, of what you experienced, and what you learned. See the gifts that that person has already brought you and look for the lessons you have learned by this person being in your life. Honour each and every person who has crossed your path and know they were placed in your life for a reason.

Chapter 6

Haters Gonna Hate

"It ain't how hard you get hit, it's how hard you can get hit and keep moving forward."
– Rocky

Many times during a divorce, a particular person or group of people can offer you resistance and challenges on top of your impending divorce. They can come in the form of a friend turned ex-friend, a group of people, an in-law, a co-worker or co-workers, or an outspoken community member. However uncomfortable this is, they have been placed in your life at this particular moment. I will share some pointers with you, as you will need to know ways to deal with these adversaries as they present themselves to you along your path. Soon, you will not be bothered by the big bad wolf, because when you are finished, there will be no way for him to blow your house down.

My friend Brenda shared a story with me of an experience she had in her local post office. She is able to laugh about it now, but when she was going through her divorce, it was instances like that that nearly threw her over the edge. Various people along the way treated her as though she were their enemy and their foe. I think it is a good thing that Brenda has a sense of humour and a vivid imagination, as you will see. I recount her story in dialogue form as it is just too funny not to. I chuckle at her antics and description, but not for what she experienced. She told me of many other instances similar to this that made me shake my head.

Joan and Jackie were busy stuffing flyers into the mailboxes down at the post office on Main Street when Brenda opened the door to the lobby. Brenda knew they saw her come in, but neither of them acknowledged that she was there.

"Hello ladies," Brenda said. "I was wondering if I could get a few stamps." Brenda stood there waiting for one of them to respond. They were clearly ignoring her.

"Excuse me ladies, but I need to get a stamp or two," Brenda said with an annoyed look on her face.

Jackie joined Brenda at the counter, but didn't make any eye contact. She just stood there. Brenda repeated herself one more time, except this time, she spoke a little louder, just to make sure Jackie heard her.

"I said, can I get a few stamps for this envelope, please?" She emphasized the please a little more than she had intended.

Jackie looked up at her for the first time since Brenda entered the building. They both stared at one another for what seemed like minutes, but Brenda refused to look away. Brenda knew she wasn't going to leave until she had her dang stamps.

Jackie mustered up the energy to open her lips and sarcastically ask Brenda, "How many stamps would you like?"

Jackie then placed her hands on the counter and stared directly at Brenda. Brenda stared back. Another minute went by before Brenda's imagination took over and she created a Western scene in her mind. Brenda imagined slowly backing away from the counter, keeping a deep and concentrated glare at Jackie. Once there was a good distance between the two women, Brenda saw herself putting both hands into her pockets. She heard music playing in the background and as she widened her stance, locked in her gaze, she said to

Jackie, "Go ahead, make my day." Brenda had been through so much crap during her divorce that I am sure her imagination and sense of humour kept her from going crazy.

"Brenda, here are the stamps you wanted," Jackie yelled as Brenda brought her attention back to the counter. Brenda was laughing as she paid for her stamps. She looked at Jackie while she licked the back of them and then stuck them to the envelope. "Be sure to send this out with the morning mail please." Brenda smirked and then walked out the door, but not before she looked back, gave a little wink, and said, "Have a nice day."

During the course of our lives, there will be many times that an adversary or foe will appear to join us on particular parts of our journey.

Despite how uncomfortable or unpleasant this experience can be, there must be some reason that this happens. Similar to the way plots of movies are developed, there is a specific moment when the villain or adversary appears. This appearance sets the scene for the challenges and adversity that the main character must face and overcome throughout the remainder of the movie. It can be the best part of the movie, the most gripping, the most captivating, and the most inspiring. You are sitting on the edge of your seat, waiting to discover how the hero will prevail over his arch-enemy.

You are anticipating what creative and dangerous techniques the hero will use, and you are most curious about who the hero becomes in order to triumph. It is all very exciting and riveting. However, when that adversary and those challenges are presented to you along your own life's journey, it doesn't feel so exciting, captivating, or inspiring.

A lot of people will admit that this process is the most difficult of any journey. Those fans in the stand who are not cheering for you, those opponents who want to see you tumble, those competitors that want to triumph over you, and that wicked witch who insists on raining on your parade. Of course, opponents are a necessary part of any sport that you play; that's the name of the game. You position yourself against an opponent to see who will come out on top and win the prize. But in life, you don't necessarily get to pick your opponents. They seem to appear out of nowhere, and, undoubtedly, when you least expect it. And the list of adversaries continues to grow and change and surprise you as you move through life.

Coming to the realization that not everyone wants to see you happy or succeed can be very daunting. You will also realize that you can't please everybody. Not everybody wants to be your friend. Not everybody is going to agree with you or see life the way you do. Not everybody is in your corner. Not everybody is a fan of yours. Everybody does not love Raymond!

There are a variety of situations that can be a breeding ground for an opponent to appear. My client, Arlene, discovered that for herself when she was given a promotion at work and became the supervisor. One particular employee at the office was not happy about Arlene's promotion and the authority that Arlene had over her. The work environment became toxic and almost unbearable for Arlene. The employee took every opportunity she could to point out Arlene's mistakes, which made Arlene nervous and contributed to her making even more mistakes. There were constant confrontations, ensuing arguments, and an office that soon became divided.

Arlene began experiencing headaches, and just the thought of going to the office created anxiety for her. She was at the end of her rope, and she was considering quitting her job. I suggested that she ask this woman out for lunch. It would give them an opportunity to talk in an environment outside of the office and to talk about something other than work. Arlene would be able to express her concerns about how she was being treated and would consider alternate solutions if this did not work out. Arlene needed to tell her how she felt and to let her know that this was not going to carry on any longer. Although this made Arlene feel uncomfortable, she agreed to give it a try. After a lengthy conversation, Arlene discovered that this employee was jealous of her promotion because she had been overlooked for that position. She thought that if she gave Arlene a hard time that maybe Arlene would quit. She obviously didn't realize how strong Arlene was, and until that moment, Arlene didn't know how strong she was either.

I know that it does not always work out as it did for Arlene, and that the adversaries you are facing may be a lot more aggressive or vocal about their disapproval of you. They may make it very well known how they feel about you, and you are tired of having to deal with them all the time. It has taken its toll on you and you find yourself, once again, avoiding certain places in order to avoid possible confrontation and outbursts. Sometimes they are unavoidable as you run into them often at your children's events or other places around town. As unnerving as it feels, you won't be able to avoid them forever. I know that, throughout your divorce, there may have been many times when you lost your cool, got scared, and shrunk in the face of those who came to dislike you. It may not be easy at the moment, but after the heat has turned down, there is always an opportunity to choose a different response.

Arlene's story reminded me of a young man who I know who showed me how to physically face an opponent head-on. It is hard for me to forget the feelings I experienced watching my son fight inside of a cage as an MMA fighter. I describe it as feeling every single emotion that exists all at once. Despite the nerve-racking emotions, what stood out the most for me was the moment he walked straight toward his opponent, unwaveringly, greeted him at the centre of the ring, and stared him in the eyes. He wasn't going to back away from him. He summoned all of his courage, all of his strength, and gave it all he had. He was not going to let this guy take him out of the game.

I learned a lot from watching my son in that cage. There are circumstances and moments in your life when you are called upon to take a stand for yourself. There comes a time when you must face whatever challenges or adversity that is before you head on. Your divorce has offered a great challenge for you, and it is summoning you to dig deep and find out what you are made of. The time has come to take action rather than spending any more time in your head trying to figure out why this is happening. Why are they doing this to you, and why now? Do you want to know why you and why now? Because that's what's happening. There is no deeper philosophical reason than that. You are going to rise up, face your challenges, and get your life moving in a new direction.

Let me share with you the longest five steps that I have ever taken. You might be thinking that those five difficult steps were taken when I was eleven months old and first learning to walk. Or maybe you think those difficult steps were taken when I was five years old and entering the kinder-garten classroom on my first day of school and realized that I had forgotten my crayons on the school bus. Perhaps you are convinced that the longest five steps that I have ever taken were the last five steps of a 42.2K marathon that I completed when I was forty-seven (42.2k is equal to 110,800 steps). You would be incorrect if you thought that any of the above situations even came close to being the most difficult. Five of the longest and most difficult steps I had to take were the steps leading into the lobby of the local hockey rink where my two sons played hockey. My feet felt like they were full of lead, my legs were trembling, my vision was blurry, and my stomach was turned upside down. What could possibly be at the top of those stairs that would have me so worked up? My small-town adversaries. Despite how I felt, I walked right through them and into the stands to watch the game.

Sometimes, that's all you need to do. Stand up tall, be proud, and look your naysayers in the eye. Let them see that you are not afraid of them and that you are not going to back down. Their actions, words, and opinions do not hold a candle to the strength, will, and determination inside of you. Like an MMA match, you can honor the strength in your opponent without shrinking the greatness inside of you. You playing small does not serve the world.

And now it's your turn. In order for you to face your adversaries, you will need to start practicing. We are going to have some fun as you choose a particular foe that you have been avoiding. Instead of avoiding places that you might run into this individual, you are going to seek them out and stand in their presence. And, on the days that you are feeling extra brave, you are going to say hi to them. If the way they look at you makes you feel small and timid, then you are going to build that muscle and stay right where you are and feel the strength inside of you.

I love supporting my clients as they find the capacity within themselves to face, challenge, and tackle the villains in their story as well as any other challenges along the way. I know that it can feel daunting and overwhelming at times, that's why we work up to this moment together. Just like my son—who was primed, coached, and supported to face his opponent,—I will help you do the same.

Chapter 7

I Haven't Any Courage...
I Even Scare Myself

*"I don't want to be at the mercy of my emotions. I want
to use them, to enjoy them, and to dominate them."*
– Oscar Wilde.

E motions can be become elevated during divorce and
for long periods of time afterward. Vulnerability,
fear, insecurity, and anger all come to the surface to
be exposed, felt, and dealt with. It can be extremely hard to
try and manage, control, and come to terms with the burst of

emotions coming at you from every direction. It can feel as though your emotions will never settle down and that you will never know a moment's peace again. You constantly feel rattled, shaken, and on the edge, ready to go to battle with whatever emotion decides to appear next.

You will read experiences that some of my clients have been through as they traveled down the emotional road of divorce. I will share exercises that I used myself as well, as I learned to wrestle with the emotions that consumed my life and my body during my divorce and afterward. You will see by the end of the chapter that you do not need to be afraid of your emotions. Your emotions may have turned up to maximum volume, but with the help of an exercise that I share with you, we will turn down that volume and have you feeling more at peace.

I will start with an emotionally excruciating event that one of my clients, Elaine, experienced unexpectedly one morning when she was on her way out of town. The retelling of her story brings to mind my own experience of watching my children in the care of another woman. I have had many parents share with me the heartache it brings up seeing their children with someone else. Although it is an inevitable and unavoidable experience, it does not take away the pain in your heart when it happens to you.

Elaine was driving past the school on her way out of town when she saw a familiar vehicle coming toward her. She became excited at the thought of seeing her son's smiling face as his dad dropped him off for school. But her excitement diminished quickly when she saw her ex-husband's girlfriend driving the truck with her son inside of it. Heat began to fill her body, starting in the very pit of her stomach. The heat rose into her chest as it became difficult for her to breathe. There was a heaviness that consumed her heart and brought tears to her eyes, making it difficult to drive. Her entire body trembled and shook at the mere sight of another woman with her child. She tried desperately to stop the tears, but the pain in her heart expanded, creating a moment that felt completely unbearable. Elaine didn't remember the drive back home, as she opened the doorway and collapsed to the floor. She couldn't recall how many hours she laid there, tending to her broken heart, allowing those feelings to have their way with her.

Divorce brings with it opportunities to feel a wide range of emotions. Life-changing events such as this open up intense feelings of anger, fear, guilt, and grief. You feel like you have been blindsided by an entourage of emotions and you struggle moment to moment trying to handle, deal, and navigate your way through the experience. You would give anything for a moment's relief. What you find is that you cannot escape these feelings, and it seems as though you will feel this way forever. I compare it to the experience of riding a rollercoaster—so, if you care to indulge, please continue forward.

Ladies and gentlemen, boys and girls, step right up—the ride is about to begin! Please keep your hands and feet in the car, fasten your seatbelts, and look straight ahead at all times. This rollercoaster is about to take you on the ride of your life, and I want you to be ready. There will be many up and downs that will have your head spinning in all directions. The sharp turns will make you want to tighten your grip and hang on for dear life. The sudden drops will turn your stomach inside out and the never-ending loops flipping you upside down and all around will make you want to scream. You may, at one point, become paralyzed with fear and beg for the ride to end. I will not be able to stop this ride once it is in motion, but I want you to know that the ride will eventually come to an end.

It is hard to imagine that people actually stand in line, pay money, and choose to go on a ride like this. To many, it sounds fun, exciting, thrilling, and packed full of adventure. Perhaps you are one of those people. Whenever you are at the fair, you line up with great anticipation to embark on this thrilling adventure. The ride is specifically designed, and you willingly take a seat to experience what lies ahead. Being with that feeling seems so much easier when you are on a rollercoaster compared to the emotions you feel living day to day. And by day to day, I mean the movements of energy that course through your body at any given time, morning, noon, or night, middle of the night, middle of the day, early morning, mid-morning, five minutes past mid-morning, five minutes before lunch, during lunch, just before you are done with your lunch, five minutes after you are done with lunch, and any time in between. These times are all possible times for intense movements of energy to take complete control over your body.

I studied meditation practices for many years, and I vividly recall the very first time I sat down to formally meditate. I started with a five-minute meditation as I felt that would be a good amount of time to sit still. About thirty seconds into the meditation, my butt wanted to get up off the chair. Five minutes felt like an eternity. I had no idea how I would ever be able to sit there for longer than a minute without going stir crazy. Over time, I was able to withstand the uncomfortable feelings that would rise up when I sat down to meditate, and now I can easily sit there for over an hour. I have found that the ability to sit with what is happening within you and around you have a huge impact on turning down the volume on your emotions.

I wanted to share this with for a few reasons. One, because if I can learn to sit still for longer than five minutes, anyone can. (This girl is like a pot full of unpopped popcorn ready to burst open at any moment.) Second, because I feel like meditation has the potential to change your emotional, physical, and psychological states, as I know it did for me. And third, because I am not going to ask you to formally meditate. If you choose to do that, I think that's great! The rollercoaster ride that I am going to invite you on at the end of this chapter will have you sitting in the cart during the ride, but you do not have to have your eyes closed, sitting cross-legged on the floor holding your fingers in a particular position for you to benefit from the experience. Follow along.

Emotions are real and raw and can be crazy intense. I have no doubt that you have experienced many moments or extended periods of time where the fear inside of you completely restricted your ability to physically move. Moments where the anger inside of you was so raw that it felt like your blood was boiling and the anger was going to blow through the top of your head. Times when you were so heartbroken that you had no idea how those pieces would ever be put back together again. And maybe even times where you found it hard to breathe, you couldn't stop the racing of your heart, and tears seemed to flow at the most inopportune times.

My friend, Sharon, and I met for coffee one afternoon because she needed a friend to talk to. She started opening up about her divorce and how things were unfolding for her and the family. Sharon was having difficulty processing all of the emotions she experienced. There was a lot of drama in the breakup and a lot that Sharon needed to deal with. She was feeling overwhelmed, lonely, and angry. As I looked around the room, there were many people who seemed curious about what we were talking about. They knew Sharon's situation, and I suspected they were conjuring up some stories to tell their neighbours. It was a sensitive moment that, unfortunately, was viewed by onlookers. Just another circumstance that makes it difficult going through a divorce in a small town.

Despite the fact that this moment contained an audience, Sharon felt safe with me to let her tears flow, as I held her hand and let her cry. She noticed when she tried to keep her emotions stuffed inside, they would get louder and louder. Do not underestimate the power of feeling your emotions and letting the waterworks flow. Rather than damming up your emotions, open the floodgates. Once the river has run dry, the volume on your emotions will have been turned down, and you will feel much more calm, relaxed, and peaceful.

When you are experiencing a flood of emotions, it is natural for you to ask why you are feeling this way. It is much the same as the onlookers from the coffee shop. They are wondering why you are crying or feeling so distraught. If they know you are going through a divorce, they may speculate that it has something to do with your ex, your children, your shortcomings, or your in-laws. They may begin to make up stories. If they are unaware of your pending divorce, they may wonder who passed away, what possession you lost, or if you are ill. In other words, they start to make up stories as they guess and wonder why you are crying. It's unfortunate that so much attention is on the "why" rather than the emotion itself. Someone is upset and struggling. Finding out what they are sad about won't change that fact. We can offer our compassion without needing to know anything about the story.

This is true for you as well. Spending any amount of time trying to get to the bottom of your emotions is precious time you could be spending feeling the emotion instead and letting it go. I know you have a million stories for me about your ex. I know you want to smack your neighbours for being so darn nosey. I know you want to lose it on your coworkers who walk around like their crap doesn't stink, and you have a word or two for all of your married friends who look down upon you because you gave up on your marriage and they didn't. Regardless of the circumstance, you and the audience at the coffee shop are going to have to come to terms with the tears that are flowing and try not to worry so much about the story.

Adding to the list of emotions that family and friends have shared with me that show up somewhere down the road of their divorce are insecurity, shame, jealousy, and guilt. Some have shared with me that it consumes them daily. I remind them that we have all mistreated others and acted in ways we wish we hadn't. I am certain that, as you are reading this right now, you, too, could come up with a list of reasons to feel guilty or bad about something. Or, maybe your mind travels in the direction of the people who have hurt you, and you feel they should feel bad, guilty, and remorseful for what they have done to you. It is a common game that is played during divorce and throughout relationships in general. Guilt runs deep as we were taught at an early age to feel bad and confess our sins.

I wonder what our daily life's experience would be if we focused on one another's best qualities and the inherent goodness within each other, rather than focusing on our shortcomings and wrongdoings. Perhaps, you think, this would be a convenient way for you to get away with your own hurtful actions towards others. Nope. You are no angel and I doubt that you profess to be. You have hurt people and you have been hurt by others. You have watched the people in your life blame and hate others who hurt them. You have watched people live with guilt and shame for their entire lives. I have a grander vision for humanity. That one day, we will live without guilt and shame and because of that, we will be able to experience the depth of joy within us. I feel that this is what we are all after, the happiness, the joy, and the love that resides within. I recall how I felt walking up the steps of the Lincoln Memorial in Washington, D.C., and as I was overwhelmed with emotion, I heard the words of Martin Luther King Jr's I Have a Dream speech. I thought to myself, I do too, Martin. I do too!

One evening when we were heading out for dinner, my friend Rodney shared with me that he was struggling with all of the guilt he was feeling. He seemed to have a million reasons for his guilt. He felt bad that he couldn't make his marriage work and felt like he had let his ex-wife down. He had guilt when he thought about his three children and was worried about how the divorce was going to affect them. His guilt intensified as he reminisced over past decisions that he had made and wished he had chosen differently on several of those moments. He recalled all of the times he had mistreated a few of his good buddies, and he even brought up the guilt he felt for how he ran his business and treated his employees.

I am sure that he could have named off another 100 reasons to feel guilty if I hadn't have stopped him there. I said to Rodney that he cannot change anything that has already happened and worrying about how his kids will turn out won't help anything either. Letting go of the past and being present with his children is the best gift he could give his kids, I reminded him. I said that he could make amends with the people who he felt he mistreated and offer a sincere and honest apology if he was indeed sorry for his actions. He was going to have to do some work on forgiving himself. Relieving the past, unfortunately, is common for people to do as they carry this baggage around for a long time, sometimes an entire lifetime. Rodney continues his journey through guilt, but has at least taken some steps to let it go.

Soon, I am going to share a method that you can use to turn down the volume on your emotions. We are going to go on a rollercoaster ride, but before I explain the method, I will show you how I used it in the following story. It is an intimate moment, but I thought I would share it with you anyway, perhaps, more than anything, to prepare you for the story about me that follows in Chapter 10. Honestly, though, I do want you to know that I have been through the same experience that you have. Our stories may be different, but the feelings that come with change, loss, and drama are all the same

I was on a date with a man I had seen on several occasions. We had a lot of fun together and I quite enjoyed his company. I am pretty sure I had made him laugh a time or two, as well. We were enjoying my favourite breakfast one morning—medium rare steak with eggs on the side—when he decided to share a deep revelation with me.

"Denise, darling," he said.

Oh boy, I already knew where this conversation was headed.

"I really enjoy spending time with you, and I love your energy, but," he stopped mid-sentence and decided to go no further with this conversation. We sat in silence for about fifteen seconds when he felt it was safe enough to continue.

"Denise," he whispered. "It seems as though you want to take your fork and stab me in the eyeball."

I waited until I regained my eyesight and the ability to form a complete sentence before I responded, "That is very observant of you." I wasn't sure if he was waiting for a chocolate chip cookie for guessing correctly, but, as you can imagine, this girl was not in the mood for cookies. I managed to keep a steady stream of oxygen flowing through my body that only seemed to fan the fire burning deep within me. Neither of us spoke until I was brave enough to muster these words. "I respect how you feel. I seem to be experiencing a rather intense movement of energy in my body." Tears formed in the corner of my eyes, so I knew I had to hurry up and get those words out before the dam burst open. "I am sure that I could come up with a lot of psychological reasons as to why I am feeling this way. I haven't known you very long, so it seems strange that I would have this type of response to what you just said." I shared one more thing with him before the flood gates opened. "What I am trying to say is that I am not going to try and figure things out. I just want to feel what I am feeling."

At that, I let it all go. I allowed myself to cry, sob, and blubber without trying to contain myself. I felt the pain in my heart until everything started to quiet down and all that remained was a puddle of mucus on my blouse. I looked over at him and smiled. I was surprised at how good I felt after having gone through what I just did. I felt lighter, happier, and proud of myself for not stabbing that fork into his flesh. We parted ways with a hug, and I have never forgotten that moment.

I call that automatic reaction in me my little spider monkey. It can rear its little head at the most interesting of times. Most people have one but may have another name for it or they convince themselves that somebody else is causing them to feel that way. It doesn't matter what the feeling is—anger, anxiety, jealousy, or fear—there isn't any of us who are exempt from these emotions. I like to call them movements of energy rather than labeling these emotions separately like there is something different we need to do depending on the emotion. Whatever you decide to call it, you will learn to become proficient at allowing this energy to move through your body and you will go easy on yourself in those moments you struggle to do so.

I read a book called Wherever You Go There You Are by Jon Kabat-Zinn. It turns out that every conversation you engage in, every place you happen to travel, every relationship you are in, and in every circumstance that appears in your life there is one common denominator: you! I found out that regardless of whether I was looking over the Grand Canyon, embarking on a new career, or living in a new town, I would find the same element in all of those places: me! It turns out that you can't run and you can't hide from the emotional blocks inside of you. You are either running from them or decorating your life in such a way as to keep yourself safe, and to try and prevent these feelings from emerging.

Regardless of what path you have chosen, I am going to invite you to allow these feelings to emerge. You will find out, just as I did, that you won't die from feeling these emotions and after the feeling has passed, you end up feeling just a little bit lighter and a little bit brighter, not a bad payoff if you ask me.

And now, it is time for you to have some fun! I want to invite you to come along on a rollercoaster ride with me. We are going to hop into that car, buckle up, and hang on until the ride is over. I know that it will feel intense, but I promise you that the ride will end at some point, and I will be right there with you. The next time you feel a strong emotion welling up in your body, imagine yourself on that rollercoaster and hang on. Let the feeling pass through you without trying to stop it. And rather than holding your breath, closing your eyes, and hoping that it will soon end, I want you to take a deep breath and enjoy the ride. Whatever feelings come up, just feel them and let them go. Sit in that car and focus on your breath. Take another deep breath and focus on that breath going up your nostrils, into your lungs, and deep into your belly. Now exhale and follow your breath the entire way, until, you have expelled all of the air out of your body.

I want you to do this for the entire ride until the cart comes to a stop and the ride is over. The invitation does not expire, so feel free to hop into that cart whenever those emotions present themselves, and just know that this too shall pass. The volume will have decreased on your emotions and you may even feel some happiness welling up inside.

Chapter 8

If Only I Had a Brain... That Didn't Think so Many Thoughts

"A man is a product of his thoughts,
what he thinks, he becomes."
– Mahatma Gandhi

I imagine, that even before your divorce, you were aware of the many thoughts that consumed your mind day and night. And now, these thoughts seem to be amplified and inescapable. They haunt you. The ones that ring the loudest are the negative thoughts that make you doubt yourself and leave you feeling insecure. We are going to discover a way for you to deal with those negative thoughts in a playful and fun way.

My friend Karissa let me in on a little secret one day. She confessed that she was seriously struggling with some dark, negative thoughts that were not only keeping her up at night, but also distracting her at work and preventing her from moving forward with her life. Karissa learned very quickly that, regardless of how crazy her life may look on the outside, nothing could compare to the battleground inside of her head. She confessed that she was constantly bombarded by a stream of thoughts that never seemed to stop. She was no stranger to a busy mind, but the divorce added a plethora of negative thoughts that she couldn't control. Karissa began noticing a nasty group of thoughts that had her doubting everything about her life. She was greeted in the morning, as soon as she woke up, with the most unpleasant thoughts like, "I am never going to get through this. I think everybody hates me. I am such a screw-up."

She said that these thoughts would stay with her all morning and then continue on as she did her shopping. "I hope my kids are going to be okay. I am the world's worst mom. I fail at everything." The harder she tried to stop them, the louder they got. When she would go for a coffee she sat there thinking, "I bet everyone is talking about me. I wish I was skinnier. I shouldn't have eaten that cinnamon bun. Maybe I need to go on a diet. I wonder if I should join the gym. You screw everything up. You deserve to be alone. Nobody wants to be with you anyway"

These thoughts mixed with all of the prior thoughts she had been thinking earlier, and by the end of the day, she felt exhausted, worn out and completely spent. She had no idea how much energy the hamster in the wheel that lived inside her head was taking up. But that hamster wasn't done yet. As soon as her head hit the pillow at night, the hamster went into overdrive until there was nothing but smoke coming out of her ears and a set of bags under her eyes to greet her in the morning and begin it all over again.

When it feels like your life has fallen apart or you have experienced a great loss and things are not like they used to be, it can be easy to fall prey to all of those nasty negative thoughts. Divorce is one of those events that can most certainly bring out the worst of the worst. Your mind will have you questioning everything about yourself. You know exactly what thoughts I am talking about. Those thoughts that tell you're a terrible parent, a loser friend, someone who always screws up, someone who will never figure it out, that you are stupid and hopeless. Those thoughts that paint nothing but a dismal picture of you as a human being, which leave you feeling lost, fearful, and hopeless. It can feel like you have fallen into a dark, deep hole, and it is difficult to see any light up ahead.

It is important to know what to do when these negative thoughts appear and start to take over your life. I am going to equip you with a cool hack to help quiet down those thoughts so you can experience a greater degree of clarity and some much-needed peace of mind. I feel grateful that I discovered a woman by the name of Byron Katie. Byron teaches a method called The Work, wherein she provides a way for you to question your thoughts and move into a new experience. I used this same process to quiet the gremlin in my head that had me doubting and judging everything about myself. I knew that quieting those thoughts was what I needed to do in order for me to move on.

I began asking if the thought "I am not good enough" was true. Most people never question the thoughts in their mind, so they end up believing everything that they hear. When I discovered that the thought wasn't true, I then got to experience what it felt like when I didn't believe that thought. Not only did I feel it, but I could also envision what was possible for me when I didn't go around believing that thought. I was able to accomplish things I once believed were impossible for me, and I felt more positive about myself and the people around me. I began my journey of letting go and felt more equipped to deal with these thoughts.

How did all of these negative thoughts come to be? Sometimes, having an understanding of how your mind was programmed with these thoughts can prevent you from going completely crazy and help you to work at dismantling the program you were wired to believe. I will give you a brief and simplified overview of how your programming came to be. I am going to keep it brief because this is exactly where people become stuck and unable to move forward. All of their focus, attention, and energy stay right here in the story. They get stuck in blame, judgment, and resentment, and that is the last thing that I want for you.

When you were growing up, it is likely that you were raised by parents or other caregivers who had negative thoughts about themselves running through their head. The likely felt unlovable and unworthy, so they parented according to those beliefs. Your parents may have unknowingly neglected you and your needs, projected their insecurities and fears unto you, or they either overprotected you or you needed protection from them. They scolded you for not doing things the right way and they would frequently mention that you were bad, naughty, and in heaps of trouble. Even when they were expressing their love or giving you their undivided attention, you unknowingly interpreted many of their words and actions as a form of disapproval, abandonment, and insecurity because of the previous messages you had been given. Now, where would your parents learn such a thing? Why, from their parents, of course, and any other social programming they were exposed to. They had the same conditioning enforced upon them as their parents did and so began an endless loop of patterns, conditioning, and belief systems installed into the minds of millions. We all became programmed with these insecurities, and now we are on the path of healing and experiencing life without them.

I have such an appreciation for my client, Joel, who was willing, after I had made the suggestion, to take a moment to question the validity of a recurring thought that he had about being an inadequate father. Up until that moment, he believed the thought as gospel truth, and he noticed that whenever he was with his children, he would interact with them in such a way to either cover up his inadequacies (by buying them gifts, taking them on vacation, or giving in to their every request) or he would be in such a dark place he would withdraw his love and attention and often ignore his children, leaving them to play on their own while he drank and watched sports on television. He admitted that he would often drink to cover up the feelings that came up when he believed these thoughts about himself.

He was ready for a change and was very eager to work through this process with me. He could see what it was creating in his life and was willing to do anything to change. I asked him if the thought that he was an inadequate dad was true or not. Joel struggled with this process because he was conditioned to believe that everything his mind was telling him was the truth.

After many sessions with Joel, he came to realize that what he was believing was not 100 percent true and, in fact, there were other, more empowering thoughts that he could choose to focus on. He began focusing on more positive thoughts like I am a great father, I am fun dad, my children love spending time with me. This new perspective and how he saw himself changed many things for him. He felt so much better about himself and walked with more confidence than he ever had before. He didn't feel the need to drink so much and began spending more quality time with all of his children. It was amazing for me to watch the changes that happened in his life.

The suggestion that I gave Joel came from Byron Katie's book called A Return to Love. The work, as she calls it, is significant in many ways and the part of life that it helped me with the most was in my personal relationships. Her work was instrumental in helping me to heal many relationships in my life, including the one with my father. As with most child/parent relationships, I was struggling, working through the many challenges that relationship presented to me. After diligently questioning my thoughts, many hard conversations, and some extra help from above, I was able to see my father in a new light, and I went on to enjoy and appreciate the love and the wisdom that he was able to share with me and many others. I felt blessed to be by his side as he took his last breath and passed on with much grace and peace. When we question our thoughts, we reprogram the beliefs we once held about the people in our lives and we begin to experience deeper and more meaningful relationships.

I had some fun with Sara and came up with a game that she could play as a way to become disentangled from her thoughts. She began by sharing with me how these thoughts were presenting themselves to her.

"I can't stop thinking the thought that I will never get it right, I always screw things up," she said. "I will be out walking my dog, or reading a great book, or lying in the sun, and my mind drifts to these thoughts. The other night, I was watching a movie with my daughter and I was so happy to finally get to see her and spend some quality time with her, but as I was sitting there snuggling with her on the sofa, my mind wouldn't stop telling me what a screw up I am. It makes it so hard to have quality time with my daughter. When she isn't with me, I miss her so much, and when she is with me, I spend most of that time beating myself up by listening to these thoughts. It doesn't seem to matter what I do; I cannot stop the incessant thinking in my head. It makes me miserable and I want it to stop!"

Sara was clearly disturbed by all of the chatter in her head. She was constantly bombarded with thoughts that made her doubt herself, her parenting abilities, and her worth as a human being. Her experience reminded me of how lost we can all get inside of our head when we give so much attention, energy, and belief to those thoughts. Sara wanted to know what she could do to stop it from happening and I told her that I didn't have a way to make the thoughts stop but what she could do was simply notice the thoughts. I made it into a game and then showed her how to play. I asked her if she was familiar with the game whack-a-mole, the game where the moles randomly pop up out of their holes and then you whack them on the head with a big old hammer. I told her to imagine those moles as thoughts that pop up in your head. Say, for example, a blue mole pops up and that blue mole represents the thought that is telling you what a crappy parent you are. You are going to notice that thought, get familiar with it. Notice what color that mole is, notice how it seemed to pop up out of nowhere when you were trying to enjoy your dinner. Notice the reaction your body is having to that mole. Your body may want to run away and hide or slam that mole back down to where it came from, so you don't have to feel any emotions that are arising alongside the thought.

I reminded Sara that the mole represents her thoughts. Rather than trying to wrestle with the thoughts that continually pop up and ignite a rollercoaster of emotions, I wanted her to imagine that she was standing in front of a whack-a-mole game and she was going to take a step back from the game and just watch all those moles popping up. Watch the game unfold but do not play the game. You will even notice the mole slide back down its hole and you didn't have to do a thing. Just watch.

Sara wasn't so sure she wanted to play. It sounded like a dumb game to her. Much like the game of chess, she felt she may lose interest and fall back into those negative thoughts. I reminded her that, like any new thing you try, it is going to feel uncomfortable and perhaps frustrating until you become more practiced and versed in the play of the game. I also reminded her that she didn't have to play, no one was going to force her, and in fact, unless she really wanted to play, unless she had a burning desire to really want to experience something other than being lost in her thoughts and allowing those thoughts to dictate how she feels and acts in the world, it won't work. And the same is true for you. Unless you give this a try, nothing will actually change.

I had always wanted to complete a marathon, but my mind was telling me that I was too old, I was out of shape, and it would be too hard. I found out that the city marathon was happening in thirteen days. Thirteen days? I knew that the only thing that would hold me back from doing this was my mind. I was sick and tired of listening to that voice in my head and believing everything it was telling me, so I decided I was going to go for it and do whatever it took to get out of my head and across that finish line.

I decided that I was going to go against my "usual and habitual" daily patterns. I was going to challenge my mind and the thoughts that seemed to dominate my experience. I messed with every part of my daily routine. I drove a different route to work and parked in a different stall every day. I never once walked in the same direction, pattern, park, or area of the city. I listened to every type of music imaginable, slept on the couch, floor, and spare bed. I normally do everything with my right hand, so I did as many tasks as possible with my left. I ate dinner meals for breakfast, oatmeal for lunch, and I even drank various beverages at oddball times of the day. Wine for breakfast is an interesting way to start your day! I went to bed at different times, and I never once set my alarm for the same time.

A few days into this experience, my mind was confused. It was used to having its way with me and telling me who I was, how I would be doing things, and how the day would unfold according to the limits and patterns it previously set for me. I was challenging each and every thought, and toward the end of the thirteen days, it felt as though my mind surrendered to me. It was a lot more quiet than usual, and at one point, it felt as though I didn't know who I really was. It stopped yelling and screaming at me. It stopped expelling its opinions and views and yielding to me. The morning of the marathon, I told it what was going to happen that day. I told my mind I was going to complete a marathon and there was nothing that it could say that would interfere with me doing that.

Words of wisdom that a mentor of mine once shared with me were either you ride the donkey, or the donkey rides you. In other words: either you are in control of the mind, or your mind will control you. I was definitely riding the donkey! I lined up with the other participants and began a twenty-year-long dream. My mind had little to say about it. It had been whipped into place during the last thirteen days and knew better than to give me any sass. I wasn't going to listen to anything it had to say, and I certainly wasn't about to obey the crap it had gotten into the habit of spitting out.

I tell you this story for a few reasons.

1. To let you know that you really do have the ability to gain control of your mind.
2. To show you what is possible when you learn to disengage from your thoughts.
3. To give you a fun experiment to try yourself to quiet that pesky critic inside of your head.

As promised, I have given you several suggestions for you to play with to quiet that mind of yours. I would love for you to share your experiences with me as I hope you have some fun with this. Now get to it, and go ride that donkey!

Chapter 9

That Change Will Do You Good

*"Nothing is so painful to the human mind as a
quick and sudden change."*
– Mary W Shelley.

D ivorce is certain to bring about an enormous
amount of change in your life. Nothing is the same.
Your marital status has changed, obviously; you
are no longer someone's husband or wife. You don't have
the same friends, live in the same house, or see your children on a regular basis. You may encounter a different job or

career, and your financial situation can become uncertain or unstable. Your in-laws may no longer be a part of your life, or certainly not like they used to be. Everything about your daily routine is different, new, and uncomfortable. Living with this change can be overwhelming, to say the least.

You desire to become more comfortable with the changes in your life and to feel more at ease as things continue to change around you. I will share stories that involve some changes that were brought about by seeking the changes, and then other stories that speak about the changes in our lives that happen very suddenly and unexpectedly. Your comfort will come from a perspective shift when you begin to shine a light on the parts of your life that light you up. I will explain that to you at the end of this chapter, so please stick with me, and let's embrace these changes together.

I have witnessed the impact that such dramatic and quick changes can have both in the lives of my clients and personally in my own life. Divorce brings so many changes to your life and it can take time to adjust to your new way of living. Until I was able to accept the changes and stop going back to the way things used to be, I struggled and fought with finding a new way to do life. You feel heartbroken for the way life used to be, and you miss some of the people who are no longer in your life. You feel scared about the uncertainty that lies ahead, and you feel anxious and lost without the usual contact and routine that you were so accustomed to.

Divorce is not unlike experiencing death when it comes to changes and the alterations that occur in your daily routine and other areas of your life. Although, when you divorce, it is treated differently by others, compared to how they respond when you experience a death in your family.

My father passed away several months ago, and I am watching my mom adjust to all of the changes in her life. She misses having someone to talk to, and she has no one waiting for her when she comes home after completing her errands downtown. She was used to having someone there to tell her funny jokes and long stories. Her meal preparation has changed; she is making all of the decisions and dad isn't there to kiss her goodnight and enjoy some physical touch. Some furniture in the house changed and his belongings are no longer there. These changes are difficult to adjust to, and she knows that each season brings even more changes. My mom is learning to do things on her own.

Overcoming how uncomfortable it feels to do things differently or to try new things you have never experienced before is a major hurdle for many people to jump over. Getting excited about new things and going to different places can help ease the hole you feel inside and help you to adjust to a new way of living. Change is difficult regardless of how it is brought about in your life. Your willingness has a lot to do with how quickly you will adjust and will determine the quality of your experiences.

Change can feel more manageable when we bring about that change deliberately. For example, you tell your hairdresser that you would like a drastic makeover. You cut, color, perm, puff, straighten, streak, braid, bun, shave, or extend your hair. It can take a bit of getting used to, but for the most part, this change is fun and exciting. It brings a new energy and some spunk to your step. You were happy to get rid of the old hairdo and update to a new one, and you love the results of that change and how you feel.

You can also decide to change the ambiance of your living space. You start by painting those dull and bland white walls with a warm and inviting grey tone. You replace the worn-out carpet with a wooden flooring and a cozy throw rug in the middle of the room. You take down the blinds and drape a gorgeous material over the windows. The furniture is outdated, and you are tired of the springs in the couch poking your butt every time you sit down to watch television. A new and updated set of furniture arrives, and you and your butt couldn't be happier. You stand back and take a look at all of the changes that you made. It feels completely different and you love it! Remembering the times in your life when you invited change and you loved it can help you to appreciate some of the changes you are experiencing and struggling to adjust to.

I remember my client, Mindy, and how disoriented she was when she started her new job. She was excited to learn new skills and work in a new location with new people. However, that excitement didn't last for long. She was overwhelmed with all of the changes that took place in a short period of time. She was unsure of where anything was in the office, which did not sit well with her OCD and her need to organize things. Her new, required skills that she had not yet mastered were causing her to feel a lot of anxiety and pressure.

The new location in the industrial side of the city meant that she was commuting a longer distance than usual, and rather than being surrounded by restaurants and cozy places to grab something to eat, she was forced to pack a lunch or go hungry. Not everyone in the office was warm and inviting, and she often felt like the outsider and that maybe she didn't belong there. Too many things had changed all at once, and she was having difficulty coping with it all. I suggested to Mindy to arrange a few things at work that would quickly become familiar to her. For example, I had her organize her desk the way she liked it, as this would help to settle her need for organization, and I also suggested that she make friends with one of her coworkers, so she didn't have to feel so out of sorts and unfamiliar with everything. Jumping in as she did, and arranging what she could, helped her to adjust to the changes that were out of her control. Although Mindy was struggling with the changes at work, I am sure you can relate to the difficulty of her change as it relates to your divorce.

Although you find yourself amongst radical change, see if you can keep a routine that you are familiar with. It may seem insignificant, but holding on to a few familiar objects or ways of doing things can help to diminish fear as you look around your new environment. You can find comfort in the things that have stayed the same and the things you enjoy to help you embrace the things that have changed and the things you find less enjoyable.

Mark was not unlike Mindy, except for the fact that, on top of coping with the changes brought about from a new job, he was also going through a divorce at the same time. He was juggling his new work schedule with the scheduled time with his children. He had moved into a different home and needed to adjust to this new living space. His brother-in-law who was once his best friend was no longer there for moral support, and his usual over-active social life was now non-existent as he began spending more time on his own. He was learning to cook for one when his children were not with him, and on top of everything, he missed his dog. He, too, was looking for some answers and ways of dealing with the changes in his life.

What I had both Mindy and Mark do was to begin taking life one day at a time. Trying to figure it all out in one day was not going to happen, so they needed to give themselves time to adjust. Rather than focusing on what life was going to look like in a year from now or how they were going to handle next week, they just needed to focus on the day they were in and take it as it comes. I asked them to take note of the positive things that were happening in their life, similar to the way a gratitude journal works. Place your attention on the people, places, and things you are enjoying and that are making you happy. What you focus on, you tend to create more of.

I have compassion for people experiencing such dramatic changes, as I know it is not an easy process and can bring with it a lot of uncomfortable and painful feelings. It is good to remind yourself that change is a natural and inevitable part of life. You haven't done anything wrong and you are not being punished because your life has been shaken up. Often, changes are brought about in order for you to grow as you learn to navigate new environments and evolve into the person who can adapt, accept, and thrive in an ever-changing world. You have within you an innate ability to weather the storm, accept these changes as a natural part of life, and perceive these changes through a different set of eyes.

Remember, you are up against your mind, which wants to keep you safe and protect you. The best way that it knows how to do this is to keep things the same. When things are changing, the mind is having to constantly access the environment and look into its database for information on how to keep you alive. It will fight for you to keep the status quo, to do the same things that you did yesterday, and it will pull on the reins when any movement is made towards something new or different.

In order to combat all this change, let's pull out that flashlight so we can shed some light on the beautiful things occurring in your life. Once again, let's have some fun. This is my version of a gratitude journal. Rather than writing down what you are grateful for, I want you to take a flashlight and shine it on all of the things that make you smile, the things you appreciate, the things that you love, and the things that make you happy to be alive. Yes, I am serious. Actually use a flashlight. I encourage you to carry a small flashlight with you so you can do this regardless of where you are. Why am I asking you to use a flashlight? Because, once you are done carrying that flashlight around with you, you are going to replace that flashlight with your eyes! Yes, your eyes. You will come to associate appreciation and gratitude with everything you lay your eyes on.

A change in perception is a very powerful way to walk through the changes in your life. Appreciating the positive things that are happening in your life now does not dismiss the positive and wonderful things that were occurring in your life before, but it does prevent you from remaining stuck on the "way things used to be," and not enjoying or appreciating what you have now. It is also a great way to empower yourself. We are not often in control of the outer circumstances that are occurring around us or of what other people say or do. But you do have control of how you react and respond to these changes.

One of my favourite movies is *Pleasantville*. It is such a great example of how drab, boring, dull, colorless, and predictable life would be without change. In the beginning, it appears to be so comfortable and "pleasant" to know how things will turn out, how your daily life will unfold and how nothing out of the ordinary will happen. It is amazing to watch what happens when things start to change, when something is done differently, when change becomes acceptable, and when some color is added to the scene. It's as though the lives of these characters begin to transform, and life projects them into a colorful, passionate, and ever-changing 3D reality of life. I know that change is uncomfortable but there is a colorful, passionate 3D reality life waiting for you to embrace and enjoy, now go get it!

Chapter 10

I Have a Feeling We're Not in Kansas Anymore

*"The quest for certainty blocks the search for
meaning. Uncertainty is the very condition
to impel man to unfold his powers."*
– Erich Fromm

L ife is like a box of chocolates—you never know what
you're going to get. Ain't that the flipping truth! You
can wake up one morning, and life is heading you
down a particular path, and then whammy! You get smacked

up the side of the head and all of a sudden, your life has taken a 180. You are in the land of Oz and it's filled with munchkins, witches, scarecrows, and a yellow brick road, and you have no clue where that road leads, what the scarecrow wants from you, or what the heck these munchkins are doing in your story. It is daunting. It is terrifying. And it can leave you feeling paralyzed and unable to move forward.

Waking up one morning and finding yourself without a spouse, without your children, living in a different home, surrounded by different friends, working at a different job, can leave you feeling uncertain and extremely vulnerable. You are uncertain about everything. You felt certain that you would be married forever, and now you are divorced. You were feeling certain that you would be living in your home for many more years, and now you're not. Life is unfolding in many unexpected ways, and you find yourself needing stability and certainty in an almost desperate way. You would do anything to create a life that you could predict and know how it turns out. Well, we know that we cannot predict how things will turn out, but we can get you more comfortable with uncertainty and maybe even get you to laugh at vulnerability, or least laugh at how it can show up.

I love the analogy of movies to describe the uncertainty of how things play out in life. You arrive at the theater, excited to watch your favourite actor take to the big screen to play out a hero's journey. You have a sense of what the movie is about because you watched the trailer, of course, but you have no idea what is about to happen, how it is going to make you feel, or how the whole thing is going to end. That uncertainty is exactly what brought you there, and it is that uncertainty that built up enough excitement and curiosity inside of you to make you want to go.

You did not show up at the movie theatre because you wanted the person beside you to give you a play-by-play of what was going to happen before it happens. Who the heck shows up for that? I don't want them spoiling all of my fun. I don't want them taking away the thrill and excitement of not knowing how it's about to go down. You showed up for this movie to be surprised, delighted, relieved, thrilled, held in suspense, disappointed, heartbroken, elated, shocked, bewildered, and captivated.

If we can get excited enough to immerse ourselves in the uncertainty of a movie, why are we so anxious about the uncertainty in our own lives? Why do we show up to a movie for all those crazy experiences, yet run for the hills when that uncertainty shows up in our lives? What makes the uncertainty of a movie more desirable, exciting, and thrilling than our own uncertainty? It is our own conditioning and the fact that someone, or a lot of people, along the way, taught us to be afraid of the unknown. They painted a scary picture of all the possible outcomes, and you figured that perhaps it is best to not enter any unknown territory willingly, lest you lose your life. Again, your mind just wants to keep you alive, so it is going to strongly resist anything unknown.

It always comes down to that, doesn't it? Every "what if" story that is played out to the end always ends in death. Someone will surely die, and that someone is usually you. Your mind races to create all sorts of elaborate, colorful, and very convincing scenarios of what will surely happen next. Wait a minute. Doesn't that sound familiar? It is the exact same thing as the play-by-play loudmouth sitting beside you in the movie theatre. He has never seen the movie and he has no idea how it is going to turn out, yet he takes it upon himself to shout out all the possibilities and inevitabilities that he can imagine, and it is usually something negative that is going to happen. Annoying! Guess what—your mind is doing the same thing, and likely the people around you are voicing their own fear of that unknown circumstance.

Feeling vulnerable and exposed as you dance through the changes and challenges of your divorce are very common feelings. Clients that I have worked with have found it difficult to allow themselves to feel vulnerable as they fear ever having to feel the same deep emotional pain that their divorce brought to the surface.

Randy had been divorced for over a year and happened to lay eyes on a beautiful woman that he wanted to ask out on a date. This had Randy all worked up. We had been friends for years, and I had never seen him like this before. His wife had left him, and he was feeling especially unsure about himself. He could hardly stand the nervousness he felt as he decided he would approach her and ask her out. He knew that if he was to ever be in a relationship again, he was going to have to take some chances and be vulnerable. He finally got the question to roll off his tongue, and to his delight, she said yes.

The best antidote that I have found to combat vulnerability is to face it head-on. It isn't something that you can escape, and trying to avoid it leads to a very secluded life that will have you trying to outrun this moment every chance you get. When you realize that asking someone on a date, feeling embarrassed, reaching for a goal, exposing your truth, and engaging in the difficult conversations isn't going to kill you, it does get easier.

I will tell you the following story to assure you that I have faced fear and I know what it is like to feel vulnerable. I was caught off guard one day while driving home to my small town returning from the city. The gas stations are few and far between, and the little towns that do have gas stations often close before the sun goes down. Was I filled with fear? Did I have a lot of emotions coursing through my body? You can bet your sweet petunias I did. It wasn't that I feared running out of gas. In fact, I was running on a full tank. But I did need a bathroom, and the fear was real, as it was very clear to me that I wasn't going to make it. I would not be using a toilet for this disposal (and I didn't need to pee!). I didn't quite make it to the side of the hill in that straw field along that dirt road. As I squatted there, knowing that I would never wear that dress again, I knew that if I ever wrote a book, I would have a great story about the most vulnerable moment of my life. Squatting in that straw field, naked as a jaybird, watching an old farmer drive by and nearly have a stroke upon seeing this strange specimen in his field, I knew that if I could survive this moment, there wasn't anything that I couldn't get through.

This call to vulnerability is not for the faint of heart, and I happen to believe that no one is born with a faint heart. I believe that you are born with everything you need in order to be with each and every moment, and everything that happens at that moment. All of the adventure, all of the surprise, and all of the possibilities are right here waiting for you, calling out to you, and begging you to come closer. I recently returned from a 6000-kilometer road trip with my nephew. It was a rather spontaneous decision, which was made the moment I saw that Chicago was a city we would be passing through to get to Washington DC. What made this trip adventuresome, fun, and exciting, besides the fact that he got to travel with his favourite aunt, was that we were throwing caution to the wind and taking the trip moment by moment. We did not plan and decide things ahead of time. We were uncertain as to where we were going to stay, what events we would take in, or where we were going to sleep. This allowed us to crash a wedding in Chicago at our hotel (can you say photobomb?), meet a well-known reality television actress (I knew something was fishy when she had 286,000 followers), experience some unique buildings, bars, and brothels (just kidding about the brothel, I couldn't think of another b-word and that just sounded funny to me), attend our first ever NBA game in Chicago (a lot of magic happened there), saw the cherry blossoms in bloom (ain't that a pretty sight?), got a ride in a police car (don't ask), and many other delightful adventures that would not have happened if we were unwilling to open ourselves to new experiences, despite being uncertain and unsure of how things were going to go. We were willing to meet new people and just be ourselves.

Being open and exposing yourself takes some bravery. You would rather keep a wall around your heart—protect your vulnerabilities and insecurities—than take a chance on this moment. This feels rather "safe," but it prevents you from experiencing this moment the way it really is. Not the way your mind is telling you, but the way it is unfolding right now at this moment. If you are wondering how to stay open, just don't close. We had so many opportunities on our road trip to experience the moment as real and raw, unplanned and unscripted, and as fresh and free as it gets.

After experiencing many painful moments in your life, it can feel almost natural for you to guard, shield, and protect your heart from ever experiencing this type of pain again. But doing that also prevents you from experiencing the love, the joy the beauty, and the excitement that is available to you at this moment. I like this quote from Criss Jami, "To show your weakness is to make yourself vulnerable. To make yourself vulnerable is to show your greatest strength." Many humans try to hide their weaknesses, their faults, and the very obstacles in life that they struggle with. It is only when you show those aspects of yourself that your greatest strength is revealed. Then, having that strength to build upon, you stop hiding, you stop playing small, you start loving yourself, and you start loving others just the way they are.

I invite my clients as often as I can to experiment with this exercise, which usually creates an uncomfortable feeling of vulnerability. There are necessary conversations that we need to have with people in our lives. Many of these conversations are avoided because we fear the other person's reaction or response; we fear the outcome and we fear the feelings that will surface, either for ourselves, the other, or both. But avoiding these conversations is not helping anyone. It doesn't solve anything, nor does it allow the individuals to express their truth or resolve their issues. I have always said that having the hard conversations is one of the hardest things to do, but can also bring the greatest rewards.

I am not offering a suggestion for you to call someone and give them a piece of your mind. Often, a hard conversation involves letting someone you know how much you love and appreciate them. It involves apologizing for a behaviour or an absence of behaviour that hurt them, and it can involve inviting the other person to share their feelings without you judging or trying to edit their experience. It is not as hard for people to engage in a conversation where they are blaming, judging or condemning the other person in some way. Decide right now who you would like to make amends with, who you would like to ask how they are feeling, or someone who you haven't connected with in a long time and you feel inspired to reach out to. I am sure that there is a family member or a friend that would love to hear from you! And remember, this is meant to be fun!

Chapter 11

There's No Place like Home

"Who you are is not an option. You are love.
It hurts to believe that you're other than
who you are, to live any story less than love."
– Byron Katie

We have arrived at the last step that you will embrace before we finish this part of our journey together. There is one final suggestion that I would like to make in order for you to feel complete. You have travelled a great distance with me, and I hope that you have been implementing the tools and hints that I have made in order for you to cultivate the strength, vision, and perspective necessary to hold your head high and move forward with confidence.

What's next for you? You have survived the drama of a divorce, and now it is time for you to move onward and upward. But what does that mean, and where are you meant to go? What does it mean to move on? Are you meant to move away, marry a new honey, buy yourself a dog, or maybe take up knitting? (Don't laugh, but I actually bought myself some knitting needles. They are collecting dust under my bed.) I am not for or against any of those things. I am going to suggest that you don't need to "do" anything. The moving on we are going to do here is an emotional and mental moving on.

Remember when Dorothy finally made it to the Emerald City where the Wizard of Oz resided? Well, just like Dorothy, you have come a long way. You can be pleased with yourself for having overcome so many adversities, for having to leave some friends behind, and making some new ones along the way. You withstood the rumours of how you were responsible for killing the wicked witch or other such deeds. You learned to overcome fear and those annoying negative thoughts in your head. Someone must have used the tools that I just wrote about.

But wait a minute! The moment Toto peels back the curtains, Dorothy realizes that the Wizard isn't really who she thought he was. He was all smoke and mirrors, creating an illusion that made her believe that he had some sort of power to help her get back home. She believed with all of her might that he held all of the magic, that he would be the one to help her to get home, and that he had some sort of power that she didn't. But she discovered he was nothing more than a sweet elderly man, likely reliving his childhood. Dorothy was a lot like you, perhaps, doubting you have what it takes inside of you to get to where you want to go. The old man behind the curtain was all smoke and mirrors, so I guess it's up to you, darling.

Dorothy is now faced with questioning everything about her journey. If the Wizard was an illusion, what other parts of her journey were illusions as well? Did the rumours and gossip actually exist the way you thought they did? Were people really talking about you as much as you thought they were? Were the things that people said congruent to who you really are? I mean, I know that Dorothy wasn't perfect. She likely stole a few cookies from her aunt's cookie jar, she most likely said a few cuss words under her breath, and I highly doubt she was faithful to her daily chores on the farm, but did the Wicked Witch and all her little men need to chit chat about her human error? I am most certain that, those uttering her inadequacies were equally aware of their own, isn't that what makes us all human? To err is human—I think I read that somewhere once. That means if you are a human, you will be making some errors along the way. Well, if that's the case, I guess there is no need for a crucifixion.

And all of those "friends" that headed South as soon the weather cooled down, how good of friends were they anyway, and did they have more to teach you by leaving rather than sticking around? Were those the people you wanted or needed in your corner? Perhaps their season was up, and as soon the leaves started falling from the trees, that was their cue to exit stage left. Dorothy seemed to find some pretty darn loyal friends along the way that supported her, encouraged her, and loved her just the way she was, lost and all!

Let us not forget about the "adversaries." You know, those wicked witches that stared her down, those angry little men that didn't want her raining on their parade, and don't forget all of those characters that took it upon themselves to let her know she wasn't welcome in their land. What was their purpose in the story? The journey back home down the yellow brick road was tough enough without people placing land mines, setting off bombs, and throwing hand grenades at her. But would she have become the woman she needed to become in order to find the Wizard of Oz without all of that? It seems as though all of the stuff they threw at her only made her stronger, more resilient, and much more courageous and determined to get to where she needs to get to. Let us give thanks for those that make us stronger in their own unique and special way. What doesn't kill you makes you stronger; this I know!

How about all of those negative thoughts and self-doubt that you had to contend with? Or those thoughts that were trying to convince you that you were not good enough and that you were never going to make it? You ended up discovering that those thoughts were not even true. Who knew? They sure seemed convincing. When you hear the same thoughts over and over and over again, it is a little hard not to validate them. Unless you muster up the courage to question their truthfulness and find a deeper truth for yourself. A deeper truth that you are so much more than the thoughts in your head. It turns out that when you simply observe your thoughts, they don't even faze you. They can't harm you, and they don't stick around very long either.

Dorothy's friend fear came along for the ride and did its best to scare the crap out of her every chance it could. Your fear multiplied with all of the changes you had to endure and all of the uncertainty you had to face. And perhaps the greatest thing you learned along the way was that you needed to be vulnerable and open your heart so that this moment would show you the way back home. It was at that moment you were told you had had the power within you all along.

If Dorothy didn't have the guidance and support she had along the way, I don't know how long it would have taken her to find her way back home, or if she would have made it at all. I know that the same is true for myself. I was familiar with a lot of information and techniques, but when it came to applying them to my life situation, my conditioning made it extremely difficult to implement and follow through with. I had an amazing coach who I worked with to go through the process of writing this book, and I know for certain that I am not the same person who began writing it. During my divorce, I also sought some outside guidance to help me navigate my way through the process.

When you are feeling lost and uncertain, you can become lethargic in your decision making, addictive in your behaviour, and self-sabotaging in your actions. Those around you end up feeling those effects, while your relationships, career, and health are jeopardized. You end up spinning your tires or feeling like a hamster in a wheel, doing a lot of running around but not really getting anywhere. Perhaps some forward movement is made, but without putting those beliefs into check, they rear their head again and again and again.

The opportunity to experience your daily life in a completely different way is absolutely possible. I have shared some activities for you to engage in, the opportunity to view people and situations from a new perspective, and ways for you to be with your busy mind. I know how these activities have served my own life as well as the lives of the people that I have worked with. It is all there for you to experience and to enjoy the freedom on the other side!

For our last fun activity together, I want you to invest in some self-love. It may be easy for you to shower those around you with compliments and acts of kindness, but how often do you do that for yourself? How often do you compliment yourself? At some point in the day, you will likely find yourself in front of a mirror. I want you to take a good look at who is looking back at you. Look her in the eyes, and let her know how amazing and beautiful she is. Shower her with praise for what she has already overcome and for what she has accomplished. Let her know that you are proud of her and that you have all the faith in the world in her to accomplish whatever she sets out to do. Remember, you are love, and it hurts to believe otherwise.

Chapter 12

You Are Not Alone

"I don't want excuses. I know what you are up against. We're all of us up against something. You better make up your mind, because until you have the balls to look me straight in the eye and tell me this is all you deserve, I am not letting you fail. Even if that means coming to your house every night until you finish the work. Do you understand me? I see you! And you are not failing."
– Erin Gruwell, *Freedom Writers*

Yep, that's how I feel! I am not going to let you fail. I don't want anything less for you than you deserve, and I am not going to quit until we get to where you want to go. Now, I don't know if I will come over to your house, unless, of course, you live somewhere warm and close to the ocean (I just survived thirty days of negative forty degrees Celsius weather, so I may consider this as an option). I know who you are and the capacity that you have inside of you. I also know that you have been through a lot and you have experienced a lot of pain. You have been holding back and are ready to move forward.

After surviving a divorce, it can be a struggle to pick up all of the pieces (not even all the king's horses or all the king's men could put Humpty Dumpty back together again), so please don't feel bad about where you are right now or how you are feeling. The mind is determined to keep you safe, so it will keep running the same programs it always has, despite your best efforts to go against it. It seems to get louder and double its efforts to keep you safe when it sees that you are wanting to make some changes. It is not that you are incapable—I have all of the confidence in the world in you—I just know that you are programmed for survival and your body is going to do everything it can to keep you where you are.

Randy is an intelligent man who studied many spiritual teachings and who attended many self-help workshops and programs. He gathered a plethora of mantras, meditations, information, insights, tools, techniques, and tricks along the way. He could quote many great teachers, recite the science behind human behaviour, and he even had the inside scoop on many energy healing modalities. Despite all of this information and all of the tools that he accumulated and hung in his shed, he wasn't actually using these tools to plant, maintain, or cultivate his own garden of growth. After we had worked together for many months, consistently implementing the steps outlined in this book, he noticed a difference in his daily experiences. His life showed what he learned, rather than him telling the world what he knew. He became closer to his daughter after actually having the hard conversations he put off for so long. He was able to start a business project that he kept avoiding because he listened to that voice in his head that was telling him he wasn't good enough. He diligently questioned those thoughts and began believing in himself again. He experienced a lot more joy and ease in his life. There is no better feeling than seeing the tangible and emotional ways in which someone's life changes after applying the knowledge they have learned.

There will be days you feel unmotivated and you can easily convince yourself that you just don't have what it takes. The outside influences of life can put a damper on your spirits and make it easy for you to say, "Maybe tomorrow." Or worse yet, allow you to settle. You know that gnawing feeling in the pit of your stomach that just knows you have something more inside of you, that living with all of this fear, doubt, and guilt is not how you are meant to live out the rest of your days? You feel it, you know it, and perhaps that's why you picked up this book.

Experiencing what is on the other side of all that noise inside of you is so rewarding. Being able to move forward with confidence, experiencing less anxiety and stress, and having an increase in the amount of energy in your body is worth the challenge to work through it all. Crossing the finish line of my first marathon after I diligently challenged all those thoughts in my head that said I couldn't do it, or when I finished the first draft of this book—when I never imagined being able to complete such a project—changed so much in my life. It changed how I see myself, how I feel about myself, and what I feel is possible for my life and the people in my life.

I don't want to see you going around in circles, chasing a tail that you will never catch. I do not want to see you going through life knowing you have more to give and never allowing that part of you to come out and play. Life is short, so why not make a commitment right now to make the best investment you will ever make? That investment is in you!

The stock market, your real estate investments, or whatever rate of return you are getting on your money will never touch the return you will receive when you invest in yourself.

Dying with a spark inside of you that never had a chance to sparkle is one of the greatest tragedies there is. It is tough to watch a loved one die, to see the end of a marriage or a career, or the deterioration of your health, but to permit those circumstances to be the excuse you use to not move forward in the best and brightest way possible is the tragedy. Life is going to do what life is going to do, and so much of it is out of your control.

Please stop thinking that you are alone in this or that you have to figure all of this out on your own. You are not alone and there is help, love, and support here for you. I would not be who I am today if it were not for the coaches and mentors I invested in along my journey. Whatever you decide and however you choose to work through this, I will honour you and I will love you.

If we happen not to connect in any way other than this book, please know that I appreciate you investing your time to read it. Hopefully, you have gained some new insights and perspectives that will help to move your life forward in positive and exciting ways. And if you decide that you would like to take an even bigger step and explore what is on the other side of the mountain, we are going to have some fun together! It will be an honour and privilege to work with you as I can see us enjoying some laughter and creating some wonderful things for your future.

Chapter 13

You've Always Had the Power My Dear

"The flower that blooms in adversity
is the most beautiful of all."
– The Emperor of Mulan

I know that you have been through a lot. You are almost there. Just a few more humps and bumps to overcome, and you will be on your way. You may have struggled with a few of the suggestions that I gave you, or maybe you didn't even try. Or maybe you have decided that you could use some extra help to get you across the finish line. Yes, you have survived what feels like multiple gunshots to the body and been seemingly stabbed in the heart by family, friends, and foes. People talked about you, judged you, and offered their unsolicited opinions and views. Friends chose to walk a path that you were not a part of, and there were those chosen few who played the role as adversary in order for you to dig down deep and find out what you are made of. You are no stranger to fear and uncertainty, and to your surprise, you are still standing.

You made it this far. Perhaps you are able to walk down the streets of your town with your head held high, and you are more than happy to flip your adversaries the bird. But what if there is something more than that for you? What if it wasn't really their judgment or criticism that was holding you back? What if they weren't the ones that planted the self-doubt deep inside of you and they weren't the ones creating the fear, insecurity, and uncertainty?

You have come such a long way and I am so proud of any effort you made to implement the suggestions in this book. As I said, I really do hope that you feel better about yourself and that you have some extra bounce to your step. I am sure that feels good considering what you just went through. But I want more than that for you. I want you to discover a greater value within yourself that isn't reliant on what other people think or what other people say about you.

I have worked with clients who, on the outside, appear to have it all. Great looks, great health, and great wealth, but let me tell you, the river runs deep on this stuff. The belief that they hold about themselves not being good enough, that they are stupid, unworthy, and unlovable, often gets revealed during a difficult experience in life, if one chooses to become aware of these thoughts. Everything falls apart. It is heart-breaking to be able to see the brilliance and light that shines inside each and every person, yet they experience each day believing and living these thoughts.

The most heart-breaking of all for me was the day my nephew committed suicide. Anthony was a handsome, funny, intelligent, and loving young man. He made everyone around him laugh and he dazzled us all with his charm, his wit, and his smile. Anthony loved his family and we loved him. He struggled with these same thoughts and he had difficulty going beyond the self-limiting thoughts that plagued his mind. It was beyond sad to have to say goodbye. His passing aroused a deep urge within me to reach out to others and offer a way for them to work through the thoughts, the feelings, and the fears that weigh so heavy on them and bring them down.

Those desiring to hold their head high:

- Are ready to stop letting the gossip and opinions of others dictate how they feel?
- Are ready to let go of the relationships that no longer serve them?
- Are ready to open up to bigger possibilities beyond the fear they are experiencing?
- Are ready to be undisturbed by the thoughts in their head?
- Are ready to become more playful and fun as they journey through the drama of life?

You may be thinking right now that this is going to be tough, and I am not going to lie, it is not a walk in the park. You have been listening to those thoughts for a very long time, and your mind is going to strongly insist that you keep things exactly as they are. But I know that you have it in you to go beyond these thoughts to create the life you want. You can tell yourself it is going to be hard, or you can roll up your sleeves and learn to play the game.

I challenged my mind and completed my first marathon within thirteen days of deciding to do so. And I have learned to dance with drama and use it as a springboard to create the life I desire.

Don't listen to the words and opinions of others, you have it in you to move forward and become the best version of you possible.

Thank You!

So, did you play along?

I invited you to have some fun with me as you traveled through my book. I would love for you to send me the ideas you came up with to change up your daily routine. I am always looking for new ideas for myself and to share with my clients, as well. I would also love to hear what you are shining your light on as you go through your day. There has to be some fun or new things that you discovered to appreciate. Shoot your ideas to denise.anderson@sasktel.net.

Thank you for reading my book! As a way of saying thank you, I want to offer you a free companion class that goes along with this book. The class will support you in holding your head high as you move on from your small-town divorce. To sign up, just hop on to my site at www.deniseanderson.net.

Many blessings,
Denise Anderson

About the Author

D enise J. Anderson is a certified life coach who has been creating a simple and clear path to personal power for over twelve years. Her time spent as a financial planner, art dealer, and spiritual intuitive created opportunities for her to not only speak to large audiences, but to also travel and connect to a wide variety of people and places. She discovered a commonality amongst people that holds them back and keeps them imprisoned in their own minds.

Her first book, *Small Town Drama*—which describes the nuances of divorcing in a small town—lays the foundation for the experience she evokes during her workshops and public talks. Her own personal path of self-discovery with spiritual teachers, coaches, and mentors has served not only her personal growth, but her coaching success, as well. Denise has helped hundreds of clients to go beyond their current life situation and painful past to a more fulfilling, purposeful, and passionate place. And speaking of passion, energy, and spunk, there is no lack of that coming from this woman. She exudes her passion in everything she does, and she freely expresses the love and compassion she holds in her heart.